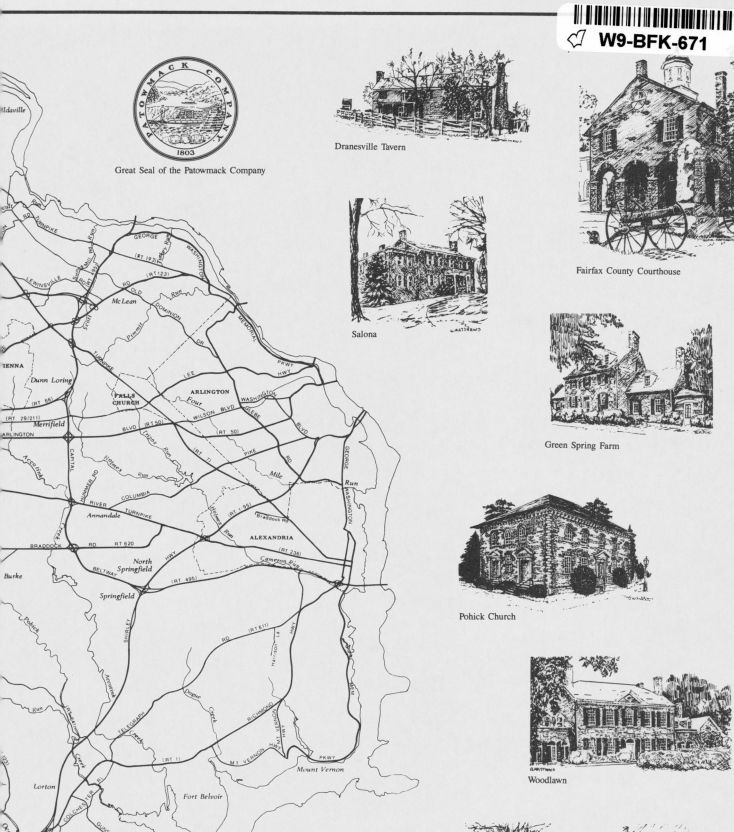

Great Seal of the Patowmack Company

Dranesville Tavern

Fairfax County Courthouse

Salona

Green Spring Farm

Pohick Church

Woodlawn

Mount Vernon

Layout by Doug Smith

Fairfax County
in Virginia:
A PICTORIAL HISTORY

THE
DONNING COMPANY
PUBLISHERS
NORFOLK/VIRGINIA BEACH

Fairfax County
in Virginia:
A PICTORIAL HISTORY

by Ross and Nan Netherton

Design by
Paula Hennigan Phillips

The Donning Company/Publishers
5659 Virginia Beach Boulevard
Norfolk, Virginia 23502

Edited by Charles S. Pierce, Jr.

Library of Congress Cataloging-in-Publication Data

Netherton, Ross De Witt, 1918-
    Fairfax County in Virginia.
    Bibliography: p.
    Includes index.
    1. Fairfax County (Va.)—History—Pictorial works.
2. Fairfax County (Va.)—Description and travel—Views.
I. Netherton, Nan. II. Title
F232-F2N47   1986   975.5'291   83-9066
ISBN 0-89865-319-3
        0-89865-429-7 (pbk.)

Printed in the United States of America

Contents

Acknowledgments

The authors are grateful to our diligent and perceptive readers who reviewed the manuscript text for this book and made valuable suggestions. Our special thanks go to Edith Sprouse, Jill Decker, William Klene, Virginia Peters, Michael Johnson, Sue Henry and Edmund Castillo for their efforts.

We were very fortunate in having available for this book the work of a large number of gifted photographers, both professional and amateur. Photographs by the following people appear in the book: Charles Baptie, William Edmund Barrett, Bernard Boston, David Clem, Abbie Edwards, Marcia Fram, Jack Hiller, Marie Kisner, Warren Mattox, Steven Moss, Gordon Mothes, David Netherton, Richard Netherton, James Pickerell, Quentin Porter, Jane Robinson, Virginia Ruck, Marvin Simms, Tuan Tran, Tom Welle, Tracy Woodward, and Carl Zitzman.

People and organizations generously loaned photographs from their collections and provided information. Included were the Alexandria-Washington Lodge No. 22, A.F. & A.M., Alexandria; Sara Collins, Arlington County Libraries; A. Smith Bowman Distillery; William Arnold, Helen Buckley, and Virginia and Lee Ruck, Town of Clifton; Edward R. Carr Associates; Fairfax County Chamber of Commerce; Lilla Richards, Fairfax County Federation of Citizens Associations; Alfred Savia, Fairfax County Fire and Rescue Services; Elizabeth David, Fairfax County Heritage Resources; Fred Beales, Fairfax County Mapping Service; Stephen Lopez, and Jay Linard, Fairfax County Office of Comprehensive Planning; Scott Boatright, Fairfax County Police Department; Fairfax County Public Library Photographic Archive; Fairfax County Public Schools; Fairfax Hospital; Ellen Anderson, Fairfax Symphony Orchestra; Harry E. Wells, City of Falls Church; Falls Church Historical Commission; Public Affairs Office, George Mason University; George Washington Bicentennial Center; George Washington Masonic National Memorial Association, Alexandria; Walter Goetz; John Gott; J. Berkley Green, Herndon; Louise Stockdale and Bennie Brown, Gunston Hall; H. H. Harwood, Jr.; Richard Stephenson, Geography and Map Division, and Mary Ison, Prints and Photos, Library of Congress; Edwin Lynch Associates; Lorraine Foulds, Media General Cable; Montebello Associates; Anne Eberle, Claude Moore Colonial Farm at Turkey Run; John Rhodehamel and Nancy Emison, Mount Vernon Ladies' Association of the Union; Museum of Early Southern Decorative Arts, Winston-Salem, North Carolina; National Archives; National Gallery of Art; James Putman, National Park Service;

Linda Bynum, Northern Virginia Community College; Dorothy Werner, Northern Virginia Regional Park Authority; Patrick Henry Branch Library, Vienna; Reston Land Corporation; Donie Rieger; Jeanne Rust; Louise McNair Ryder; William Smith; Melvin Lee Steadman, Jr.; Eleanor Lee Templeman; Frederick Tilp; United States Department of the Interior; Governor's Office, Commonwealth of Virginia; Albert Coates, Jr., Virginia Department of Highways and Transportation; Virginia Historical Society; Timothy Heigh and Robert Clay, Virginia State Library; Washington and Lee University; Washington Metropolitan Area Transit Authority; Ames Williams; Williams College; Henry Francis du Pont Winterthur Museum; and Yale University Art Gallery.

The work of four area artists appears with their permission: the *Fairfax Courthouse,* by Gloria Matthews; *St. Mary's Church at Fairfax Station* and *Clifton High School,* by Gerald Hennesy; *Vienna Elementary School,* by David Paul Skidiak; and *Belvoir Mansion,* by Nadine Sloan.

Ronald Petersen of Vienna skillfully copied and printed dozens of borrowed photographs for us. Jack Hiller took photographs and also made copies of others.

As is always the case with a work which requires a good deal of research, we were able to find resources and people at various repositories. Suzanne Levy, Eric Grundset, Karen Ann Moore, and Anita Ramos, all staff members at the Virginia Room in Fairfax County's Public Library, have been helpful, patient, and always resourceful as we searched for pictures and answers to hundreds of questions about the county's history. Anna Rups helped us at the Falls Church Public Library. Edward Russell supplied necessary facts at the Fort Belvoir Engineers Museum, and James Hoofnagle explained the new technology which has transformed the courthouse and its legal recordkeeping procedures.

Beth Mitchell supplied colonial tobacco brands and did some searching in the land records, as did Constance Ring. W. Clement Jacobs, former clerk to the School Board, furnished information about the school administration. Joseph Beard, Virginia Greear, and Elma Ellmore supplied history of the Herndon area.

Finally, the manuscript was expertly prepared by Carol Dunlap. Proofreading and preparation of the index were accomplished with the help of Verna McFeaters, Nancy Netherton, and Margaretha Backers-Netherton.

Ross and Nan Netherton

Foreword

History means the mingling of two elements, duration and place. More to the point, we may say that history takes *places*. The "where" of events is as important as the "when."

Local history obviously entails focussing upon a specific place. There are difficulties for every scale of historical writing. Global scholarship of the Spengler or Toynbee variety often suffers from grandiose theories as to the rise and fall of civilizations—generalizations so loosely big that they do not seem to fit any one society to which we try to apply them. At the other extreme, histories of very small areas tend to be unduly parochial, like local newspapers that only mention earthshaking events when they come within the ken of someone in the family of a subscriber ("FAIRFAX MAN LANDS IN NORMANDY"). Such parish-pump narratives can be endearing, but in their amateurishness they hardly qualify as serious history.

This is a pity. For many of us, and rightly, local history is the starting point. Perhaps I can be forgiven a personal example. I grew up in the north of England and went to a grammar school in Newcastle-on-Tyne. We had a splendid history teacher who inspired generations of boys. He did this by leading us on excursions. We explored the physical survivals of the city's heritage, from the traces of Roman occupation to the engineering feats of the Industrial Revolution. Eventually he produced an excellent volume on the history of Newcastle. What he did was, in a way, to turn us into *believers*. We had hitherto not truly, excitedly believed that the stuff in the history books had all occurred, somewhere, to people for whom the past was in fact the living present.

Ever since then I have been convinced that one's own neighborhood or region ought to be shown, recorded, and explained to schoolchildren, in order to impart to them the miracle of conjoining time-and-place, uniquely in their locale. Growing older (and older and older . . .), I have also come to feel that adults too can benefit from and enjoy this informed awareness of yesteryear.

The history in question need not be very remote in time. Nor need it be unduly solemn. Photographs of twenty or thirty years back can be fascinating historical documents. *Were automobiles really so curvaceous? How peculiar the hairstyles and skirt lengths of a generation ago!* Since photography has existed for almost a century and a half, there is now a rich treasury of visual material, "historical" and yet wonderfully "immediate" in impact, awaiting the alert researcher. A good pictorial history, viewed merely as entertainment, combines the appeal of family albums, yearbooks, parades, and pageants.

If the history is well done, it can not merely divert us but offer a genuine contribution to historical understanding. As the Scots say, the mickle makes the muckle. The big picture depends upon a multitude of smaller ones; without them, in the realm of historical scholarship, a broad synthesis is impossible.

However, considerable skill is called for to produce good local history. It requires a grasp of state and national as well as neighborhood events; for the muckle itself often reciprocally shapes the mickle. It demands enterprise and thoroughness in research. And, to come to Ross and Nan Netherton's

volume, a county is harder to cover than a single town or city. Fairfax County, moreover, has rarely been left to its own isolated devices. Its story is intermingled with that of the Potomac River; of George Washington and other great figures; of the evolution of the nation's capital; and of the painful, complex tug of loyalties during the Civil War years.

Ross and Nan Netherton strike me as admirably qualified for the job. They are a husband-and-wife team of skilled historians who have already done extensive work in the history of the region. They display a professional sophistication in dealing with history on the national level. Their prose is lucid, succinct, and cliché-free (which is more than can be said, alas, of many a practitioner of history); and they have assembled a remarkably large and diverse collection of illustrations, embracing some 400 years in the endlessly eventful life of Fairfax County, Virginia. I wish my old history teacher were alive today to appreciate what they have done.

Marcus Cunliffe

Flowing quietly toward Chesapeake Bay in a broad estuary, the Potomac forms the northern and eastern boundaries of Fairfax County. Numerous sheltered coves and the mouths of smaller streams —locally called "runs"—indent the river's shoreline.

The county's southern boundary is formed by the Occoquan River and Bull Run. Today many miles of the north banks of this river and stream are preserved in a natural setting in the Mason Neck area by the Northern Virginia Regional Park Authority, which has bought the land or obtained rights to protect the environmental quality and scenic beauty of the river setting. Air Survey Corporation photo, 1982; courtesy of Washington Metropolitan Council of Governments

The Land and the River

The land and the river have profoundly influenced the course of Fairfax County's history. The river gave easy access to the bounty of Chesapeake Bay and the lands along its shorelines. It served as a direct east-west route from the Bay through the Blue Ridge to the Shenandoah Valley. Indians named the river Potomac, which was translated from the Algonquin dialect as "the place where something is brought" or the trading place (Gutheim, *Potomac*).

The physical features of the land and river strengthened the character of the locale as a meeting place. The fall line of the Potomac is at the Little Falls, and it forced those using the river as a water route to break their journey and change their mode of travel. It also marks the transition from the Tidewater region to the Piedmont, making Fairfax County almost evenly divided between these two geographic regions. Here the

dense forests of the interior—so thick that men said a squirrel could travel all the way to the Mississippi without touching the ground—gave way to tidal plain, bordered with marshlands and crossed by the river's numerous estuaries and tributary creeks.

This character was reflected in the variety of natural features and wildlife found in the region. The area that now is Fairfax County was from the beginning of its habitation a meeting place of the northern and southern species of plants, animals, and birds.

Amid this natural diversity the Potomac was a unifying force, serving as a means of moving across the area easily and providing access to some of its most hidden sites. The Indians used the river corridor as the migrating wildlife had, and when the English came they followed the paths of the Indians along the streams and the river. The river continued in this way to be a unifying influence through the colonial period. After that, other forces directed Maryland and Virginia into different ways of life, and by the time of the Civil War the Potomac became one of the distinctive dividing lines between North and South.

As time went on, man-made paths of steel rails, and later strips of concrete, replaced the river corridor and the overland trails, and the area's natural history appeared to be all but forgotten in the drive to rebuild its fortunes and meet the challenge of rapid growth. But in modern times, as urbanization and economic development shape the lifestyle of Northern Virginia, the river and the land have again become unifying forces through local and regional systems of parks, parkways, lakes, nature preserves, and sources of water.

In the forest wilderness that originally covered the land from the Chesapeake Bay across the Appalachian Mountains there were thousands of bald eagles. The Potomac region was especially favorable for them because of its ready supply of fish, and of the many tall evergreens for nesting. Bold and strong, the bald eagle came to symbolize the high-soaring spirits of Americans. During the War for Independence, George Washington first used the eagle in an official seal, and in 1782 it was adopted as the new nation's symbol. Today Mason Neck provides nesting grounds for bald eagles in a natural habitat, and is the only National Wildlife Refuge established specifically for the protection of our national symbol, the bald eagle. Courtesy of U.S. Department of the Interior Fish and Wildlife Service

The Great Falls of the Potomac are the largest in a series of rocky falls and cataracts by which the river drops seventy-five feet over a two-mile distance. It is a formidable barrier to navigation of the river from Tidewater country to the lands and waters of the west. Yet the dream of making the Potomac a corridor of commerce to the great inland empire of the Ohio Valley persisted for three centuries after settlement of Northern Virginia. National Park Service photo; courtesy of Eleanor Lee Templeman and Arlington County Library

The Potomac corridor from Chesapeake Bay to the Blue Ridge follows a line dividing the northern species of plants and wildlife from the southern species. Northern Virginia thus offers an environment that is cordial to an unusually wide range of trees, flowers, plants, animals, fish, and birds. As the English settlers came and multiplied, the habitats of the largest animals and the most fragile species often were destroyed. So, today, where herds of bison once roamed, it is possible to find only an occasional deer. Other survivors of Northern Virginia's original numerous wildlife are the descendants of the smaller animals— opossum, raccoon, turkeys, and sometimes a fox. In all seasons of the year this rich heritage may be seen in the Mason Neck National Wildlife Refuge, Mason Neck State Park and Potomac Shoreline Regional Park. This unique blend of upland forest, low boggy areas, and river-front marsh, provides natural habitats for a diversity of native animals and birds. In spring and fall, the refuge is a nesting place for migratory waterfowl—the whistling swan, Canada geese, mallard ducks, teal, and others. These views from Mason Neck show white-tailed deer at the edge of a forest clearing, a white egret on a fallen tree in the marsh, and tracks of wild turkeys in the winter snow. Photo of egret by Jane Robinson; other photos courtesy of Northern Virginia Regional Park Authority

Harriot described and John White drew pictures of the Virginia Indians fishing in their rivers, which, they reported, contained a great variety of fish not then known in England or continental Europe. Complimenting the Indians for their skill in fishing, Harriot remarked: "Doubtless it is a pleasant sight to see the people, sometimes wading, and going sometimes sailing on those Rivers, which are shallow and not deep, free from all care of heaping up Riches for their posterity, content with their State, and living friendly together of those things which God of his bounty hath given unto them" (Harriot, Virginia). Courtesy of Virginia State Library

Indians and Englishmen: 1600-1740

For a century following the landing at Jamestown, Indians and Englishmen lived together in Virginia. They did not always live in peace, and their ways of life were irreconcilable in many respects. By the middle of the eighteenth century, the contest between these two societies was approaching its final crisis—the French and Indian War—each side moving under the momentum of its traditional attitudes, without attempting to understand the other's mind.

Our knowledge of the Indian era of Virginia's history is sketchy, but archeological research has found evidence of an Indian culture along the Potomac shores that was more than 11,000 years old when the English arrived. At the beginning of the seventeenth century, these people were far from being degraded savages. They had reached the highest stage of neolithic culture and mastered the secrets of

making both the land and the river yield up a comfortable living. No one can read Captain John Smith's description of his encounters with these Indians or see them through the contemporary drawings of John White without feeling some admiration, if not attraction, for their way of life.

In the area of present Fairfax County the first English explorers identified three tribes—the Dogues, Anacostins, and Piscataways—although there apparently was little to distinguish between the latter two groups. These tribes were affiliated with the Powhatan Chiefdom centered in the region of the Pamunkey Indians along the James River. But the influence of Powhatan had begun to wane as the English arrived, and the villages along the Potomac were dominated by more powerful tribes to the north, the Susquehannocks, Sioux, and, beyond them, the Iroquois

Confederation which since about 1540 had dominated the Piedmont and Appalachian regions of the east down to the Carolinas.

The Iroquois regarded the great forests of Virginia's Piedmont and Shenandoah Valley as their hunting preserve. When the first Englishmen asked what lay beyond the Blue Ridge, the river Indians replied, "The Sun," for none of them had dared go there to see. And even the English traders and settlers did not venture into these forests and highlands of the Iroquois hunting grounds for almost a century after John Smith's time.

In the seventeenth century, English settlement crept from Jamestown northward along Chesapeake Bay, seeking first the good locations along the rivers—the James, the York, and the Potomac. By mid-century land patents were being sought in the vicinity of Occoquan River, and in 1654 the first patent along the Potomac shore north of Great Hunting Creek, the future site of Alexandria, was issued to a "Mrs. Margaret Brent, Gent." (Mitchell, *Grants*).

Englishmen were interested in acquiring land, and the proprietary system provided land on condition that a grantee settle it himself or with others who worked the land for him. The steady movement up the Northern Neck therefore brought settlement which gradually pushed the Indians out. The Indian wars and reprisal raids of the seventeenth century always left the Indians weaker, but possibly more damaging was the steady deterioration of the habitat of the wildlife of stream and forest on which the Indian's way of life relied. And, most frightful of all, were the new diseases which Europeans brought with them, to which the Indians had little resistance.

By the end of the seventeenth century, the Indians of the river had become little better than fugitives in the remote parts of the Northern Neck's marshes. In the eighteenth century, Englishmen would have to deal with the more formidable tribes on Virginia's frontiers, in the north the Iroquois Confederation, and in the south the Cherokees, Catawbas, and others. No one should have been surprised, for in his *Generall Historie of Virginia*, Captain John Smith reported an incident that was prophetic. On his second voyage to the Chesapeake, Smith's party was at one point attacked by Indians from the shore, and they succeeded in capturing one of the attackers. When questioned as to why they had attacked the Englishmen who had come in peace the Indian replied "that they had heard we were a people come from under the world to take their world from them" (Smith, *Generall Historie*).

In 1590 Thomas Harriot published his history of Virginia, describing the sights he saw when exploring the coast of the Carolinas and the Chesapeake Bay region. His writing was illustrated by engravings based upon the drawings of John White who had accompanied the expedition as its artist and draftsman.

Of the dugout canoes used by the Virginia Indians, Harriot wrote: "The manner of making their boats in Virginia is very wonderful. For whereas they want Instruments of iron, or other like unto ours, yet they know how to make them as handsomely, to sail with where they like in their Rivers, and to fish withall, as ours" (Harriot, Virginia). He then described in detail how the Indians felled trees by building fires at their base, and then hollowed out the inside by alternately burning the wood and scraping it with sharp shells until it was hollowed as much as desired. *Courtesy of Library of Congress*

When Englishmen first came to the site of Fairfax County, the Algonquin inhabitants of the area were of the Necostin (or Anacostin) and Dogue (or Toag or Taux) tribes. The Necostins lived at the mouth of the Anacostia River on the Maryland side and along the Virginia shore and Analostan Island (Theodore Roosevelt Island). The Dogues lived on Mason Neck and the Maryland shore of the Potomac. Both tribes were part of the Powhatan Chiefdom which in earlier years had gathered most of the Virginia Tidewater and Piedmont Indians into a loose alliance. By the seventeenth century, however, the tribes in the Potomac region were gradually pulling away in favor of alliances with the Iroquois nations of the north.

Indian life flourished along the river and the many small streams. The Indians of the Potomac Tidewater were fishermen and corn growers. Their tools were made of stone, wood, bone, and fiber. Throughout Northern Virginia, the sites of Indian villages and hunting camps still can be found, generally near streams or outcrops of flint or quartz or deposits of pottery clay. They offer abundant evidence of the Indian presence.

Throughout the seventeenth century, the virgin forest that covered the Piedmont and the Appalachian mountains was the historic hunting preserve of the Iroquois Nations, and their war parties held the Tidewater Indians in fearful respect. And even the English traders and settlers, anxious though they were to expand westward, would not venture into the forests and highlands of the Iroquois hunting grounds. Thus, the Englishmen of 1720 were almost as ignorant of what was beyond the Blue Ridge as Captain John Smith had been in his day (Harrison, Landmarks). *Courtesy of the Smithsonian Institution*

THE PORTRAICTUER OF CAPTAYNE IOHN SMITH ADMIRALL OF NEW ENGLAND.

Ætra 37
Aº 1616

These are the Lines that shew thy Face; but those
That shew thy Grace and Glory, brighter bee:
Thy Faire-Discoueries and Fowle-Overthrowes
Of Salvages, much Civilliz'd by thee
Best shew thy Spirit; and to it Glory Wyn;
So, thou art Brasse without, but Golde within.

One of the first Englishmen to describe Virginia to Europeans was Captain John Smith, whose Generall Historie of Virginia, New England and the Summer Isles *in 1624 and* True Travels and Adventures *in 1630 were read throughout the world. His writings and his exploration of the Chesapeake Bay opened the door to settlement of Northern Virginia and the Potomac River region, and his leadership of the Jamestown colony gave confidence to others to migrate to Virginia. John Lankford describes Smith's historic contribution this way: "Smith was one of the first Englishmen to see America as more than a get-rich-quick scheme. He was one of the first to fall in love with the land and to see its potential. Beyond the forests and Indian fields, Smith envisioned growing towns and cities and thriving trade and commerce. To him America was the setting for a new civilization" (Captain John Smith's America, ed. Lankford). Courtesy of Williams College, Williamstown, Massachusetts*

After Captain John Smith, ships manned by English explorers and fur traders continued to visit the Potomac to investigate its tributaries and trade with the Indians. The progress of settlement northward from the James River moved more slowly. Not until mid-century did it reach the Occoquan River, which later was to be Fairfax County's southern boundary. In 1654 a patent was issued to Margaret Brent for 700 acres north of Great Hunting Creek, encompassing most of what is now downtown Alexandria.

Margaret Brent was a remarkable woman who had settled first in Maryland and later at Aquia Creek in Virginia where she personally managed her extensive landholdings and business affairs with skill and success. In Maryland she had often appeared before the colony's authorities, and had been appointed officially to perform numerous legal functions. The colonial assembly and courts recognized her by authorizing her to add the title of Gentleman after her name, but they would not grant Mistress Margaret Brent, Gent., the right to vote despite her strong and persistent arguments for it.

Although she may have visited her land at Great Hunting Creek, it is likely that Mistress Brent satisfied her obligation to occupy the land by settling a tenant there. If so, Margaret Brent's tenant became one of the first permanent residents in Fairfax County (Mitchell, Grants). *Painting by Louis Glanzman; reproduction used with permission of the artist*

A SURVEY of the NORTHERN NECK
of VIRGINIA, being
The LANDS belonging to the R.ᵗ Honourable
THOMAS LORD FAIRFAX BARON CAMERON, bounded
by & within the Bay of Chefapoyocke and between
the Rivers Rappahannock and Potowmack:
with
The Courfes of the Rivers
RAPPAHANNOCK and POTOWMACK,
in
VIRGINIA,
as surveyed according to Order
in the Years 1736 & 1737.

A Scale of Miles 69½ in one Degree of Latitude.

John Warner's survey of the Northern Neck Proprietary, shown here, was drawn in 1737 to assist Thomas, Sixth Lord Fairfax, to defend his proprietary prerogatives against the colonial government at Williamsburg. The trouble arose when Lord Fairfax and the colonial governor began to issue grants to land in the Northern Neck. Fairfax petitioned the King to confirm his exclusive right to do this and verify the boundaries of his proprietary.

Fourteen years were spent in this litigation, and during this time Lord Fairfax returned to London so he could personally assist in bringing his case to trial before the Privy Council.

Eventually the council confirmed the proprietor's rights and the boundaries he claimed. During the years when the proprietary power was in dispute, the land grant office for the Northern Neck was closed for considerable periods of time, but this did not prevent the 1720s and '30s from being Fairfax County's biggest land boom during which numerous small grants were issued and the pattern of land settlement was established. Courtesy of Geography and Map Division, Library of Congress

CHAPTER

3

Planters and Patriots: 1740-1800

The era of planters and patriots lasted from the formation of Fairfax County in 1742 to the establishment of a special district for the national capital, carved partly from the county's territory, in 1800. As it was created in 1742, Fairfax County extended west to the Blue Ridge Mountains, but in 1757 the land west of Difficult Run became Loudoun County. Later, in 1798, this boundary was redrawn to be roughly along Sugarland Run as extended in a southwesterly direction. This period is by far the most romantic and idealized period of Fairfax County's history. It was a time when Virginia produced leaders for a new nation, and George Washington and George Mason of Fairfax County were admired throughout the world for their ideas and examples as they led the colonies on the path to independence.

In world history, Washington and Mason seem to appear suddenly. Yet they and many other leaders were products of a century and a half of colonial public service and self-government. In this process the county courts, the parish vestries, and the House of Burgesses were proving grounds for the results of their philosophical discourses and reading about the arts of government. Even the plantation system—which always was at the mercy of uncertain weather, capricious prices, and a chain of agents and brokers that often defied control—contributed to the education of Virginia's statesmen. Few experiences were as sobering as that of carrying the ultimate responsibility for the success of a farm or series of farms comprising thousands of acres and providing the livelihood of hundreds of people.

The skills of self-government were also acquired by the merchants of the towns. In Fairfax County an example of this group which was influential in the achievement of independence is John

Carlyle of Alexandria. His house, as restored by the Northern Virginia Regional Park Authority, now serves as a unique urban historical park. Through it one may view the commercial counterpart of those statesmen who combined agriculture with politics, and on whom the success of the American Revolution also turned because of their ability at fund-raising and management of the logistics of both the war and the peace that followed independence.

The colonial period also served as a proving ground for military leadership. The French and Indian War (1756-63) opened with Washington's mission to warn the French away from the forks of the Ohio in 1754 and General Braddock's ill-fated campaign of 1755. Virginians served in both expeditions, but after Braddock's defeat the full weight of defending the Appalachian frontier fell upon the young George Washington and a hastily raised regiment of Virginians.

Two decades later, the Continental Congress turned to Washington to lead the army of the colonies united for independence. In this army Washington saw some men from Northern Virginia who had served with him earlier. Many in this fledgling force that Washington commanded, however, came from the small subsistence farms that served as stepping stones to individual independence for a great many Virginia settlers. An example of this lifestyle is recreated today in the Claude Moore Colonial Farm at Turkey Run, near Langley.

During most of this period, Fairfax County's commerce and public affairs were focused in Alexandria, its seaport and seat of government. After 1800 the official connection between Alexandria and Fairfax County was severed. In the newly-created District of Columbia, the portion ceded by Virginia was known as Alexandria County and included the old town. When this land was ceded back to Virginia in 1846, it continued to be a combined town and county until 1870 when Alexandria became an independent city, and Alexandria (later Arlington) County became a separate entity.

William Fitzhugh of Chatham was the first resident owner of the Ravensworth estate and the builder of the first residence there. He was the great-grandson of William Fitzhugh, who had received the original patent from the proprietor in 1694. He is shown with his wife, Ann Randolph Fitzhugh in portraits painted by John Hesselius.

The story of Ravensworth illustrates how the great land grants of the proprietors eventually were divided as the years went by. The original 21,996-acre grant was the largest single landholding in Fairfax County. It stretched from present-day Fairfax to what is now Shirley Highway south of the Little River Turnpike. It was first divided between William Fitzhugh's two sons, William and Henry, in 1701. Neither son lived or built on his part. Henry's portion (about

12,600 acres) was broken up and sold off by his five grandsons. William's share (over 7,000 acres) descended to William, Jr., who built and lived on the estate. On his death (1809) it was divided between his son, William Henry Fitzhugh, and two daughters, Ann Randolph Craik and Mary Lee Custis. And on the death of William Henry Fitzhugh (1830) part of his estate went to his wife in trust for his niece, Mary Randolph Custis, who married Robert E. Lee. Her inheritance was divided among her children in 1874, and part of it survived as a major tract of land in Fairfax County until the mid-twentieth century (Mitchell, Grants). Portraits by John Hesselius; photographs courtesy of Mr. and Mrs. A. Smith Bowman, Jr., and Museum of Early Southern Decorative Arts, Winston-Salem, North Carolina

Thomas Fairfax, Sixth Baron of Cameron, was born at Leeds Castle in Kent, England, in 1693. He was the only proprietor to reside in Northern Virginia. His father, Thomas the Fifth Baron, had obtained the Northern Neck Proprietary through marriage to Catherine Culpeper, an heir to the original grant made by Charles II in exile in 1649 to seven friends including two Culpeper cousins.

When Lord Fairfax emigrated to Virginia in 1747, he resided at Belvoir with his cousin and proprietary agent, William Fairfax. The following year his neighbor, young George Washington, was invited to be a member of the surveying party for the proprietary lands which included over 5,200,000 acres.

In 1761 Lord Fairfax removed his land office to his new residence, Greenway Court, in the Shenandoah Valley near Winchester where he lived and issued proprietary grants until his death in 1781. The title of Seventh Lord then devolved on his younger brother, Robert, of Leeds Castle. Portrait by Joshua Reynolds; courtesy of Alexandria-Washington Lodge No. 22, A.F. & A.M., Alexandria, Virginia

No contemporary paintings or drawings of Belvoir Mansion have been found, but the picture shown is an artist's impression of how it probably looked during the period when it was owned by George William Fairfax from 1757 to the War for Independence.

The house was built in 1741 for Colonel William Fairfax, who settled first in the Bahamas and then in Salem, Massachusetts. He came to Virginia in 1734 to act as agent for his cousin, the proprietor, Thomas, Sixth Lord Fairfax.

The house was described as a brick structure of nine rooms "and suitable outhouses." In 1757 the Belvoir estate was inherited by George William Fairfax, who was a close friend of George Washington, and was his associate in several business enterprises. When he was at Mount Vernon, Washington was a frequent visitor at Belvoir (Kilmer and Sweig, Fairfax Family). Painting by Nadine Sloan, used with permission of the artist

This lightweight, two-wheeled riding chair which once belonged to Thomas, Sixth Lord Fairfax, is now the property of Mount Vernon. It is a type of vehicle which was in common use in the eighteenth century when Virginia roads were poorly marked and maintained and travel was uncomfortable and difficult. Courtesy of Mount Vernon Ladies' Association of the Union

On the grounds of Fort Belvoir are the ruins of Belvoir Mansion, which was gutted by fire in 1783 and demolished by British naval bombardment in 1814. The house was not rebuilt by the Fairfax family or the subsequent owners of the land, and its ruined foundations remained undisturbed until the site was acquired by the U.S. Government in 1910.

The first protective measure that was taken—or needed—occurred in World War I when the camp commander, Colonel Richard Park, discovered that the site was to be used as a trench warfare demonstration area. One trench had been dug (but had not damaged any of the Belvoir foundations) before orders could be issued to shift this training to another site.

During the 1930s, other camp commanders took an interest in protecting the site and doing some exploratory excavation, but the major effort to study the ruins came in the 1970s. In 1973 the Belvoir ruins were officially entered on the National Register of Historic Places. More recently the site was excavated for archeological study, and the foundations of the mansion house and other buildings were measured and mapped.

Pictured here is a scene during the archeological project, showing Fairfax County high school students digging under the supervision of professional archeologists. Many of the artifacts found in the ruins are displayed in the Engineers Museum at Fort Belvoir. Jack Hiller photo; courtesy of Fairfax County Library Photographic Archive

Thomas, Sixth Lord Fairfax, gave an estate to his cousin William Fairfax's son Bryan (later the Eighth Lord Fairfax) in 1759. On this land, north of Leesburg Pike (Route 7), Bryan built a residence called "Towlston Grange," of which the restored brick nogging and clapboard structure, pictured here as it appears today, may once have been a part. Bryan entered the ministry in 1789 and moved to Mount Eagle, near Mount Vernon. He was a minister at The Falls Church and at Christ Church in Alexandria. Nan Netherton, photo, 1971

In the Tidewater sections of Fairfax County, as in the other parts of Northern Virginia and Maryland that bordered the Chesapeake Bay, the network of natural waterways that was accessible to ocean-going ships was an extremely important advantage. In the early eighteenth century each tobacco plantation generally had its own private wharf. As the tobacco trade increased in this area from 20 million pounds of leaf in 1700 to over 100 million pounds in 1775, it was impractical to run up to each planter's wharf to load his crop. A system of public warehouses was established for centralized grading, marking, and storing tobacco to be picked up by the merchant ships, and for more efficient tax collection. Generally these warehouses were at or near the head of navigation on a stream.

This picture from William Tatham's An Historical and Practical Essay on the Culture and Commerce of Tobacco, published in 1800, shows not only typical structures on the tobacco farms but something of the ways they were used. At the top is a common style of private warehouse with tobacco hanging on a scaffold to dry and be packed and pressed into hogsheads. Thereafter storage in a plantation warehouse or, after grading and marking, in a public warehouse, completed the process (Sprouse, Colchester). Courtesy of Virginia State Library

General concern over honest weight and standard quality in the tobacco trade led in 1730 to establishment of public warehouses and inspectors for tobacco in Virginia. Under this system an inspector opened each hogshead brought to the warehouse, removed and burned the "trash" leaves, compressed the remainder, and nailed the lid back on. The hogshead was then branded with the name of the warehouse and the net weight. These markings, plus the brand of the planter, reduced some of the risk that brokers and buyers took when dealing with planters across an ocean.

The brands shown were used to mark the tobacco casks of some Fairfax County planters. From left to right, top to bottom: Marmaduke Beckwith, Benjamin Grayson, John Peake, Charles Green (minister of Truro Parish), Daniel McCarty, Lawrence Washington, Bryan Fairfax, Sampson Turley, George Mason's Dogue Plantation, George Mason's Pohick Plantation, George Mason's tobacco rents collected from others and repacked with his brand, and George Mason's Hallowing Point Plantation.

The first public warehouse in Fairfax County was constructed in 1732 on Simon Pearson's land at the foot of what afterward became Oronoco Street in Alexandria (Sprouse, Colchester). Courtesy of Beth Mitchell

Tobacco was transported from the plantation barn or storage shed to the wharf for loading on shipboard by a variety of ways. Transportation by barge or flatboat was the most efficient method, but by far the most colorful method was to haul the tobacco hogshead along one of the many "rolling roads" that connected the inland farms with the river landings where the tobacco ships from London waited to fill out their cargoes.

A typical tobacco hogshead measured about four feet in length by two and one-half feet in diameter at the head. Fully packed it weighed almost half a ton. To move such a bulky and heavy thing overland involved fitting a wooden frame around the hogshead and fixing the frame to a shaft driven through the lids at each end. A team or dragline could then be hitched to the frame and used to roll the hogshead along on its side. Many old roads in Fairfax County leading to riverside points originated as roads along which the tobacco hogsheads were rolled, and some have retained the name of "rolling road." (Sprouse, Colchester). Courtesy of the Smithsonian Institution

During the colonial era, tobacco was the cash crop and the main source of economic growth in Fairfax County as in the other parts of Virginia. The climate and fertile soil of Virginia's Tidewater and Piedmont regions were particularly favorable for tobacco cultivation and the land needed only to be cleared and planted in order to yield a crop that brought two shillings a pound for the best and eighteen pence for inferior quality in the London market. Prices fluctuated frequently.

Everywhere land was cleared by the fastest means possible, and this often meant cutting and burning off the timber or ground cover. In the fields the tobacco plants were set out between and around the stumps in whatever pattern was convenient. Northern Virginia planters tended to grow the Oronoco tobacco which stood taller in the field and had narrower leaves than the broadleaf varieties grown in southern Virginia. Seeds for the Oronoco tobacco were first brought to Virginia by English merchants trading in Venezuela. The same variety of tobacco can be seen in this recent photograph taken at Claude Moore Colonial Farm at Turkey Run. Ross Netherton photo

Fairfax County in the eighteenth century reached to the western frontier of English settlement, and on those frontiers the style of life was a striking contrast to that of the prosperous Tidewater planters. Today the Claude Moore Colonial Farm at Turkey Run in Langley offers a living view of the colonial Virginia subsistence farmer in the late eighteenth century. The farmer's house, shown here, was surrounded by a garden, a pig pen, a clearing for corn and other field crops, a few fruit trees, and a field of tobacco. With a few exceptions the tools, furniture, and utensils were handmade. The farmer's tobacco was his cash crop and medium of exchange for buying those necessities that he could not make for himself. David Clem photo; courtesy of First American Bank of Virginia

The reconstruction of George Washington's grist mill on lower Dogue Creek was begun in 1932 by the Virginia Department of Conservation and Economic Development to commemorate the bicentennial anniversary of his birth. The original structure was probably built about 1770 and was the second Washington mill on the creek. The earlier structure was farther upstream. Built of stone from the Aquia Creek quarry, the building houses machinery and the wooden undershot water wheel which is entirely enclosed.

Washington's mill ground flour for commercial markets and neighboring farms. It represents a shift in Virginia's economy from tobacco to wheat during the late eighteenth century. Additional structures which were once part of the mill complex included a cooper's shop, distillery, stalls for thirty cattle, and pens for hogs. Courtesy of Fairfax County Library Photographic Archive

John Gray, born in 1764 near the grist mill on George Washington's Dogue Run Farm (later part of Woodlawn Plantation) was typical of many small farmers who lived in the shadows of the towering figures of Virginia's leaders of the Revolution. Gray served in the Continental Army at Yorktown and then, returning home, worked occasionally in Washington's sawmill on Dogue Run. Mainly, however, he was a tenant farmer scratching out a living very much as illustrated today by the colonial farm at Turkey Run. In the 1780s and 1790s it was reported that it took a week of ploughing to earn two-and-a-half bushels of corn. Because he owned no land, Gray was excluded from voting in Virginia, so in 1795 he went west and settled in Ohio. There he lived until, in 1868, he died at age 104. Hard working, quiet and unassuming, in his later years Gray received public attention and honor annually when, as a survivor of the Revolutionary War, he was seated on the platform of his town's celebration of the Fourth of July (Sprouse, "Companions"). Courtesy of Library of Congress

Along with the county court, the vestry of the parish church was the training ground for self-government in colonial Virginia. The parish church performed many of the social services in the community, and service as a vestryman demanded a high order of leadership in local affairs.

The custom in northern Virginia was first to establish a new parish and then a new county whose boundaries were the same as the parish. In 1732 the northern part of Hamilton Parish (Prince William County) was split off at the Occoquan and Bull Run line to form Truro Parish. When Fairfax County was created in 1742, its boundaries coincided with those of Truro Parish. Thereafter until the end of the century, the rosters of vestrymen of Pohick Church (shown here), and later The Falls Church and Alexandria's Christ Church, carried the names of many leaders in the long journey to independence and nationhood (Sydnor, American Revolutionaries). Engraving from Snowden, Some Old Historic Landmarks

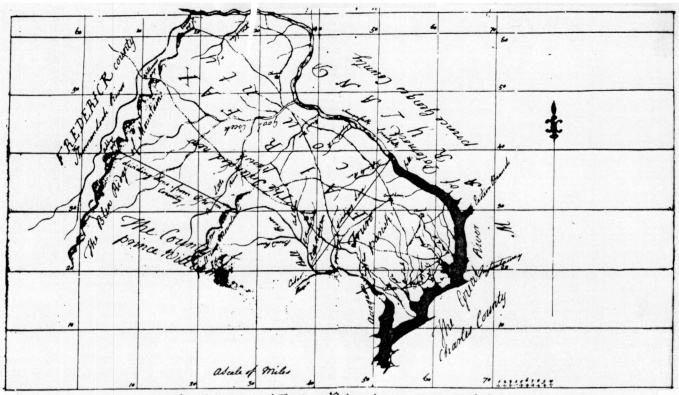

A plan of the County of Fairfax on Potomack River the Middle of which is in 39°. 12' N° Latitude

The earliest known map of Fairfax County, shown here, is thought to have been drawn between 1745 and 1748. It shows the proposed boundary line for division of Truro Parish to create a new one serving residents of the western part of the county. As shown in this map, Fairfax County extended from the Potomac and Occoquan rivers westward to the Blue Ridge Mountains. It remained this large until 1757 when the area west of Difficult Run was established as Loudoun County. Courtesy of Geography and Map Division, Library of Congress

This set of weights and measures engraved "County of Fairfax 1744" is now in the museum of the George Washington Masonic Memorial, Alexandria. Authorities in the United States and Great Britain consider this to be the oldest, most complete set of English standards extant in the world today. They were probably procured by Lord Fairfax in London before he emigrated to the county named for him. Anthony Hathaway photo; courtesy of Alexandria-Washington Lodge No. 22, A.F. & A.M., Alexandria, Virginia

Bryan Fairfax and George Washington were both born in Westmoreland County, Virginia, and were friends from their teens in Fairfax County until George, who was four years older, died in 1799. Bryan and his family moved to Belvoir in 1741 and George moved to Mount Vernon, just up the river, in 1748.

There are many entries in Washington's Diaries recording occasions when the two went fox hunting or visited together. It was at Lord Fairfax's Mount Eagle that George ate his last dinner out before his death.

Bryan Fairfax was a justice of the county court and a trustee for the roads which led from Alexandria to western Virginia, was minister of Fairfax Parish, and became the Eighth Lord Fairfax. His correspondence with Washington over a forty-five year period reveals political and social attitudes of the two men not found in other sources (A Fairfax Friendship, Sweig and David, eds). Fairfax and Washington Riding to the Hunt by F. O. C. Darley; copy courtesy of Montebello Associates

Lawrence Washington was a half brother to George Washington and fourteen years his senior. He had gone to school in England and served in the siege of Cartagena under Admiral Edward Vernon. In 1740 Augustine Washington deeded to his son Lawrence the family's Little Hunting Creek Plantation, a part of the old Nicholas Spencer/John Washington proprietary grant on the Potomac River, made in 1674. The new owner named it Mount Vernon in honor of his admiral.

Anne "Nancy" Fairfax and he were married and in 1748, George came to live with his brother and sister-in-law, leaving the home of his widowed mother near Fredericksburg.

Lawrence was an influential figure in the upper Potomac River society; he, along with several members of the Fairfax family, was an original trustee of the town of Alexandria in 1749; was elected to the House of Burgesses from Fairfax County; was owner of many slaves; and was a speculator in the Ohio Company, organized for the sale and settlement of western lands.

Soon after Lawrence died in 1752, George acquired the Mount Vernon estate by means of a release from his brother's widow (Freeman, Washington). Portrait attributed to John Wollaston; courtesy of Mount Vernon Ladies' Association of the Union

This portrait of Martha Dandridge Custis Washington was painted in 1776 by Charles Willson Peale. When she and George Washington were married in 1759, the widow of John Custis brought to the marriage tremendous wealth from the estate of her late husband which was subsequently managed by Washington in her interest, that of her surviving children, and for himself. The couple was very fond of one another and had what appeared to be an ideal, though childless, marriage.

Immediately after Washington's death in 1799, his widow burned all but two of the letters they had written to each other for forty years. Thus the most personal aspects of their relationship are lost to us.

Martha survived two husbands and four children by her first husband. She died in 1802 and was buried at Mount Vernon (Freeman, Washington). Portrait courtesy of Mount Vernon Ladies' Association of the Union

*E*dward Savage painted the George Washington family at Mount Vernon in 1790. With the couple are Martha's grandchildren, George Washington Parke Custis and Eleanor Parke Custis, who were foster children of the Washingtons. At the extreme right is Washington's valued servant William Lee, who was later provided for in Washington's will. The Potomac River appears in the background of the painting (Kinnaird, Washington). Courtesy of National Gallery of Art

*T*his portrait by Charles Willson Peale, who was a student of artists John Singleton Copley and Benjamin West, was the first made of George Washington. His wife probably arranged for the sitting, for he wrote to a friend in May 1772: "Inclination having yielded to Importunity, I am now contrary to all expectations under the hands of Mr. Peale." He added that he kept falling asleep during the sitting and therefore was worried about how the artist would represent him to the world (Washington, Writings).

Washington is shown clad in the uniform of a colonel of the Virginia Militia. It was blue with red facings, gold lace edging, and a purple sash. He wore a cocked hat called at the time a Wolfe hat. A golden gorget was suspended from his neck and he carried a sword and musket. At the time forty years of age, in addition to his military service, he had already served as a burgess, a county justice, and a parish vestryman (Kinnaird, Washington). Portrait courtesy of Washington and Lee University

The building of the Mount Vernon mansion was gradual, beginning with Lawrence Washington's modest little cottage to which George made additions in 1759, 1774, 1776, 1778, and 1787. George Washington frequently mentioned alterations to the structure in his Diaries *and in letters to friends and relatives. He connected the main house with its principal dependencies by colonnade-covered walkways (Mount Vernon,* Annual Report, 1965).*

The most striking feature of the mansion is the two-story, square-columned piazza extending the entire length of the house on the river front, an innovation which complemented the setting and accommodated the climate. The exterior finish of the main buildings was achieved by beveling heavy wooden boards and treating them with coarse sand and paint to give the appearance of stone. The entire structure seems not to have been developed under a particular architect's design or supervision (Mount Vernon, Handbook). *Courtesy of Virginia Department of Conservation and Economic Development, Richmond*

George Washington's Mount Vernon estate of over 8,000 acres was divided into five farms, each a complete unit with its overseer, workers, livestock, equipment, and buildings. It was Washington's custom, when he was at Mount Vernon, to ride daily about the farms, inspecting, supervising, and planning. In his absence this was done by his manager who sent him weekly reports and in turn received long letters of comments and instructions.

Washington was a keen observer as he traveled, and his letters often discussed crops and methods he had seen and farmers he had talked to. Despite his modesty about his "little proficiency in agriculture," he was one of the most progressive farmers of his time, and he succeeded in conserving his soil by crop rotation when others suffered the ill effects of continuous tobacco cultivation.

In spite of these efforts, the net profits *from his farms were never large, for although the four outlying farms were well managed and productive, their surpluses went to pay the annual losses on the Mansion House Farm. This latter farm was about 500 acres kept mainly in grass, groves of trees and shrubs, and gardens, as a gentleman's country estate with the master's house as the center of attention (Mount Vernon,* Handbook*). Charles Baptie photo*

The oversized bed for General and Mrs. Washington was made in Philadelphia and is decorated with reproduction white dimity hangings based on a fragment of the original. The room and its two adjoining dressing rooms are located on the second floor of the mansion above the library. The leather trunk at the end of the bed was one of Washington's favorites and it accompanied him on many campaigns (Mount Vernon, Handbook). Courtesy of Mount Vernon Ladies' Association of the Union

Throughout his lifetime, Washington kept a diary and journals and wrote over 50,000 letters, most of which survive. They are being published in a new complete edition, including outgoing and incoming correspondence, as a joint venture of the Mount Vernon Ladies' Association of the Union and the University Press of Virginia. Washington's secretary desk may be seen at Mount Vernon (The Papers of George Washington, W. W. Abbot and Dorothy Twohig, eds.). Courtesy of Mount Vernon Ladies' Association of the Union

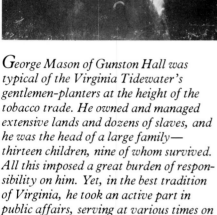

After George Mason III drowned in the Potomac, his widow sought advice from a rich merchant, William Eilbeck of Charles County, Maryland, whose property was adjacent to one of the Mason parcels of land.

In 1750 when George Mason IV of Gunston Hall was twenty-five and Ann Eilbeck, sole heir to William, was sixteen, the couple was married. Thirteen children were born of the union; nine survived. Ann died at age thirty-nine and in a poignant and long euology her husband wrote in part, "In the Beauty of her Person, & the Sweetness of her Disposition, she was equalled by few, & excelled by none of her Sex" (Rutland, George Mason). Portrait by Dominic Boudet after John Hesselius; courtesy of Gunston Hall

George Mason of Gunston Hall was typical of the Virginia Tidewater's gentlemen-planters at the height of the tobacco trade. He owned and managed extensive lands and dozens of slaves, and he was the head of a large family— thirteen children, nine of whom survived. All this imposed a great burden of responsibility on him. Yet, in the best tradition of Virginia, he took an active part in public affairs, serving at various times on the parish vestry, the county court, and in the House of Burgesses.

In all this Mason excelled and, along with Washington, emerged as a careful but forceful leader as Virginia moved toward independence. In 1775 he shipped over 50,000 pounds of tobacco from his wharf to be sold in London by his agent. A year earlier (1774) he had drafted the Fairfax Resolves, afterwards represented Fairfax County in the Virginia Convention that laid the foundation for its declaration of independence the following year, and served as ordnance officer and quartermaster for the Fairfax County militia. Physically, George Mason was short and stocky; yet intellectually and in his influence on the American Revolution, he cast the shadow of a giant (Rutland, George Mason). Painting by Dominic Boudet, circa 1811, after John Hesselius, circa 1750; courtesy of Gunston Hall

After General Edward Braddock's defeat and death near Fort Duquesne (Pittsburgh) in 1755, Virginia Governor Robert Dinwiddie appointed George Washington Colonel of the Virginia Regiment and Commander-in-Chief of all forces serving the colony against the French and Indians. The Governor directed in August that "as Winchester is the highest place of rendezvous which is exposed to the enemy, you are hereby required to make it your headquarters" (Quarles, Washington).

Washington left Mount Vernon for the assignment and within two months the situation depicted by the drawing "The appeal of the people of Winchester to Washington for protection against the French and Indians" was clearly pre-

sented in Washington's letter to John Robinson, Speaker of the House of Burgesses: "It will be necessary to observe to you that the inhabitants of this fertile and (once) populous valley, are now become our most western settlers . . .the enemy have . . .fallen upon the people of this valley and . . .a considerable part of them have already removed" (Quarles, Washington).

Washington was later elected to serve in the Virginia House of Burgesses from Fairfax County, but because he was also a landowner in Frederick County (Winchester) he first ran for and was elected a burgess from there in 1758. Courtesy of Winchester-Frederick County Historical Society

William Buckland was indentured to George Mason to finish building Gunston Hall which was completed in 1758. Because he had worked in his uncle's architectural bookstore in London, he brought to the task knowledge of the latest fashionable designs in Great Britain and Europe. His principal carver for the interior woodwork, as documented by recent research at Gunston Hall, was William Bernard Sears.

After his indenture expired, Buckland designed other dwellings in Virginia and later settled in Annapolis, Maryland. A dozen of his structures still stand there; several of them have been restored and are open to public view (Beirne, Buckland). Portrait by Charles Willson Peale; courtesy of Mabel Brady Garvan Collection, Yale University Art Gallery

Gunston Hall was the home of George Mason, who was one of the statesmen who guided Virginia to independence and statehood during the American Revolution. As was typical of a prosperous colonial planter's home, this one was located on the Potomac River, with its own wharf to accommodate oceangoing ships, and was surrounded by extensive gardens, fields, orchards, and pastures. The mansion house was the center of a cluster of buildings that housed the trades and other activities needed to operate the plantation. After being in the Mason family for many generations, Gunston Hall was acquired by Louis Hertle, who willed it to the state of Virginia under the custody of the National Society of Colonial Dames of America who have restored and refurbished it and who operate it. It is one of Virginia's outstanding museums. Courtesy of Gunston Hall

Costumed cooks prepare a meal from colonial period recipes in the kitchen at Gunston Hall. Houses such as Gunston Hall usually had their kitchens in separate buildings to minimize the danger of fire from the cooking hearth which was kept burning continuously and the discomfort of its additional heat in the summertime.

Gunston Hall's kitchen building was reconstructed in 1976 following extensive archeological excavations to find its original location, size and shape. Margaret Syfret photo, 1984

The Chinese Chippendale Room in Gunston Hall, shown here, is one of the rooms to which William Buckland gave a particularly distinctive design. George Mason started to build Gunston Hall in 1755, and later turned over the design of its porches and interior to William Buckland (Da Costa, Historic American Houses). *Courtesy of Gunston Hall*

Christmas at Gunston Hall continues to be celebrated with the traditions of colonial times. Decorated with evergreens selected from its grounds and gardens, in the evenings the candlelit house is filled with the sounds of the holiday music of two centuries ago played on musical instruments of those times. Courtesy of Gunston Hall

The Palladian Room in Gunston Hall, shown here, is named for the design of the recessed cupboards on each side of the fireplace. It is one of two rooms which are particularly distinctive, and reflects the fresh, up-to-date ideas of the architect, William Buckland. When Gunston Hall was restored in 1951, these rooms were faithfully reproduced in Buckland's design (Da Costa, Historic American Houses). *Courtesy of Gunston Hall*

John Carlyle was typical of many Scottish merchants who linked their own futures to the county's commercial centers and worked to promote the success of those towns. He was born in Carlisle, Scotland and came to Virginia as the employee of a Scottish trading firm, settling first in Dumfries in Prince William County.

In the mid-1740s, Carlyle went into business for himself and moved to the trading settlement called Belhaven on Great Hunting Creek around the new public tobacco warehouse recently established there. Here his business prospered and he gained social position by marrying Sarah Fairfax, daughter of William Fairfax of Belvoir, one of the most influential men in the colony. When the town of Alexandria was formed in 1749, John Carlyle was designated as one of its trustees and later worked to have the Fairfax County courthouse moved there.

Like some other merchants of Alexandria, he saw the risks of the tobacco trade and whenever possible he broadened his interests. So, in 1754, he obtained a commission as a Major, and an appointment as the commissary for George Washington's mission to warn the French at the forks of the Ohio to cease trespassing in areas claimed by Virginia. A year later he served as a commissary for General Braddock's ill-fated campaign against the French and Indians, and thereafter for Virginia's forces defending its western frontier. Although he became proprietor of the public tobacco warehouse at Hunting Creek, he saw Alexandria's potential as a center for exporting grain and flour to foreign ports, and he involved himself in that trade. During the 1770s, he acted as the contractor for construction of several public buildings in Alexandria. He moved in the company of the leaders of the county and the colony— Washington, Mason, Charles Broadwater, William Ramsay, John West, and others—and as the crisis with Britain developed he shared their views and joined them in signing an agreement not to import British merchandise (Harrison, Landmarks). *Courtesy of Carlyle House, Northern Virginia Regional Park Authority*

The Carlyle House, on Alexandria's Fairfax Street, is a reminder of the colonial merchants. The house was built in 1752 by John Carlyle, one of the founders of Alexandria. At the time it was the finest house in Alexandria, and in Fairfax County it was second only to William Fairfax's mansion at Belvoir.

The house is a large two-story building in the Georgian Colonial style, built of brick with stone decorative features. Along the garden side a wide terrace overlooks the Potomac waterfront. On the west front, a flight of stone steps leads to the main entrance—a double door with an elliptical fanlight and stone arch, of the keystone on which is carved Humilitate, *the motto of the Carlyle family. The interior is distinguished by fine paneled woodwork and a stairway that ascends in one continuous graceful curve.*

In the spring of 1755, John Carlyle offered his house as the temporary headquarters for General Edward Braddock while the military leader organized and equipped the British army that marched against Fort Duquesne that summer in the

opening campaign of the French and Indian War. Here, in April 1755, Braddock met with the royal governors of the five British colonies that were involved in his campaign and planned with them their strategy. Writing to his brother in Scotland, John Carlyle declared that this meeting was "the Grandest Congress ever known on this Continent."

The Carlyle House today is owned by the Northern Virginia Regional Park Authority which has restored it to the style of the 1750s (Works Progress Administration, Virginia). *Courtesy of William Smith, Alexandria*

A Declaration of Rights, made by the Representatives of the good People of Virginia, assembled in full Convention; and recommended to Posterity as the Basis and Foundation of their Government.

Thomas Jefferson, shown here at age forty-seven, was the last official visitor at Gunston Hall one week before George Mason's death on October 7, 1792. They had worked together, particularly on the Virginia Constitution of 1776, and in their last meeting they discussed fine points relative to the discussions at the Federal Convention and actions which took place there. Jefferson described Mason as being "of the first order of greatness" (Rutland, George Mason). Courtesy of Fairfax County Library Photographic Archive

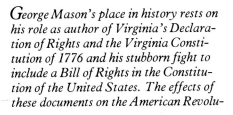

George Mason's place in history rests on his role as author of Virginia's Declaration of Rights and the Virginia Constitution of 1776 and his stubborn fight to include a Bill of Rights in the Constitution of the United States. The effects of these documents on the American Revolution went beyond the protection they provided for individual rights, for they introduced Americans to the idea of a written constitution and the principle that the people are the source of their government's powers. Courtesy of Gunston Hall

GEORGE WASHINGTON LAYING THE CORNERSTONE OF THE

Yorktown was the scene of two victories for George Washington. One was the surrender of the British army under Lord Cornwallis. The second was the final triumph over his own doubts about his ability as a commander. Keenly aware of his own lack of miliary experience when the Continental Congress appointed him to command in 1775, Washington had written to Patrick Henry: "Remember, Mr. Henry, what I now tell you: from the day that I enter upon the command of the American armies, I date my fall and the ruin of my reputation" (Dabney, Virginia).

This portrait was painted by John Trumbull in 1790 when the seat of the government was at New York, and Trumbull persuaded Washington to put on his old Continental Army uniform and ride out with him to the site he had selected to make his sketches (Kinnaird, Washington). Courtesy of the Henry Francis duPont Winterthur Museum

CAPITOL · 18 SEPTEMBER 1793 ·

Washington laid the cornerstone of the executive mansion in the Federal City in 1792 and the cornerstone of the new Capitol in 1793. In this mural in the Masonic Memorial in Alexandria, he is wearing a Masonic apron and is surrounded by government officials, family, and friends. Courtesy of George Washington Masonic National Memorial Association

Benjamin Franklin and Thomas Jefferson sent sculptor Jean Antoine Houdon from Paris in 1785 to prepare a likeness of Washington for the State of Virginia (Washington, Diaries).

The artist's full figure in marble which now stands in the rotunda of the Virginia State Capitol is the only statue sculpted during Washington's lifetime. It portrays him in military uniform, a plowshare and small implements of war around his feet, his left arm resting on a fasces.

Houdon followed Washington around Mount Vernon in an effort to catch a characteristic pose and was inspired when he saw him leaning on a fencepost arguing heatedly with someone while bargaining for a yoke of oxen (Works Progress Administration, Virginia). The statue is so accurately done that it corresponds to the subject's height—six feet, two inches) and other measurements. Courtesy of Virginia State Travel Service

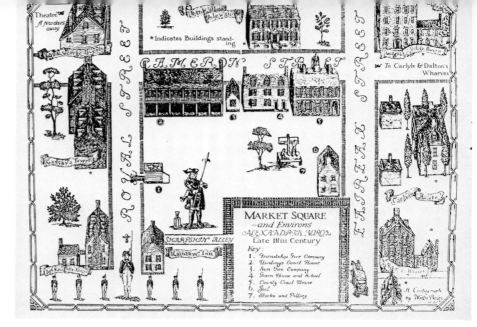

Richard Bland Lee was the first member of the House of Representatives from Northern Virginia and was responsible for the proposal that Congress establish the Federal City of Washington at its present location. He was one of three commissioners to oversee reconstruction of the government buildings destroyed in the War of 1812. In 1794, Lee built Sully plantation, a commodious country house, and a series of other buildings in the western part of Fairfax County. In his public and private life, Richard Bland Lee strongly supported internal improvement. He was active in the Patowmack Company and was a trustee of Matildaville, built on the banks of the company's canal around Great Falls. His interest in roads made way for organization of the Little River Turnpike Company, and he served as trustee of the Town of Providence in its incorporation in 1805, and of the Centreville Academy. The last years before his death in 1826 were spent as judge of the District of Columbia's Orphans Court (Gamble, Sully). Courtesy of Virginia Historical Society

Fairfax County's first courthouse was built in the 1740s near the geographical center of the county, roughly equidistant for travelers coming from Alexandria, Newgate (Centreville), or the settlements at Goose Creek. As Alexandria showed signs of becoming a prosperous seaport, however, its merchants complained about the inconvenience of the inland location of the courthouse and actively campaigned for its relocation in Alexandria with offers to contribute a site and build a new building for it.

In 1752 they prevailed and from May of that year to March 1800 the Fairfax County courthouse, together with its jail, clerk's office, and other necessary buildings, was located on Alexandria's market square at Cameron and Fairfax streets. No plans or drawings of the Alexandria courthouse have ever been found, but this cartograph shows the location of the buildings in and around the square as they might have appeared in the eighteenth century. Courtesy of Fairfax County Library Photographic Archive

Sully plantation was inherited by Richard Bland Lee, who supervised erection of its main house in 1794. The size of the farm was about 770 acres, modest in comparison with the great Tidewater plantations of earlier years, but it produced a diversified range of crops in response to the market trends of Europe and New England. The prolonged absences of Lee during his service in Congress and the hard times following the War of

Independence eventually led to the sale of the farm at auction in 1838, and again in 1841 when its buyer died heavily in debt. Its new owners, Quakers who came from the rich farm land of Dutchess County, New York, firmly believed in hard work and the new scientific farming methods and through the 1840s and 1850s the farm prospered as Fairfax County grew (Gamble, Sully). Bernie Boston photo

The tomb of the Washingtons encloses two marble sarcophagi inscribed "Washington" and "Martha, Consort of Washington." Washington's will directed that a new vault be built of brick to replace the family vault at Mount Vernon which then needed repairs and was poorly situated. Immediately after his death, Congress provided a crypt under the Capitol dome and requested permission from Mrs. Washington to allow his body to be deposited there. She agreed, but the project was never completed.

At the centennial of his birth in 1832, Congress again proposed to move Washington's remains to the Capitol. John A. Washington, his nephew and at that time owner of Mount Vernon, was urged by the legislature of Virginia not to consent to the plan. He decided to abide by his uncle's will and not disturb the remains which had just been moved to a new vault at Mount Vernon (Mount Vernon, Handbook). Courtesy of Mount Vernon Ladies' Association of the Union

When Ann Pamela Cunningham learned of the deplorable state of affairs at Mount Vernon in 1853, she decided to do something about the ruin and desolation of the home of the nation's first president. Even though Ann had been in precarious health due to an injury from a fall off her horse in her youth, she was a proud descendant of the Daltons of Alexandria who had known the Washingtons and she resolved to use all of her available strength for the cause of preservation.

Learning how to build an organization as she went along, she formed the Mount Vernon Ladies' Association of the Union in 1856 and by 1858, with the help of like-minded women throughout the nation, she had raised the $200,000 necessary to buy the estate from the heirs of John Augustine Washington, grand nephew of the great leader (Thane, Mount Vernon).

Still maintained by the Ladies' Association, in point of visitation, Mount Vernon is today first among historic houses in the nation. Portrait courtesy of Mount Vernon Ladies' Association of the Union

The newest monument at George Washington's Mount Vernon estate is a memorial to the slaves who lived and worked there. Designed by a team of Howard University architecture students, the monument consists of a tree-lined circular walk surrounding a cut-off column of stone, symbolizing strength and unfinished work. The column stands in the center of three concentric circles representing faith, hope, and love. The monument is located on the site of a small cemetery for slaves of the Washington family. Courtesy of Mount Vernon Ladies' Association of the Union

When it was opened to navigation, the Patowmack Company's canal system was heralded as the greatest engineering achievement on the North American continent, and visitors to the nation's capital journeyed up the river to see its locks. Especially awesome was the last lock opening into a chute which had been dug and blasted through the solid rock cliff. Leaving this lock the boatmen braked their progress by holding ropes tied to rings in the stone wall until at last the 60-by-6-foot gondola catapulted into a broad, smooth pool in the river below the falls. The combined drop of locks three, four, and five was 52 feet over a distance of 199 feet. The masonry walls, positions of the locks, and the sites of the holding basins are remarkably well preserved today in the Great Falls Park. Louis Childress photo from the James Watt Collection; courtesy of Fairfax County Library Photographic Archive

The Years of Growth: 1800-1861

The years 1800 to 1861 brought to Fairfax County a period of growth in every major aspect of personal and community life. Contrasts appeared everywhere. The experience of the county in the War of 1812 was anything but glorious, yet in another way the embargoes and blockades showed the county's merchants and farmers that they could draw on local natural resources and create American markets for their products.

Fairfax County lost population with the opening of the Ohio Valley, the Great Lakes region, and the prairie states beyond the Mississippi. But as some old families disappeared, new ones took their places in the migrations of Quakers and other farmers from Pennsylvania, New York, and New Jersey. These newcomers brought new methods of husbandry. Scientific farming with lime, fertilizer, deep plowing, and clover demonstrated that lands once worn out by tobacco could be restored to fertility.

American mechanical genius was released in an explosive burst of energy during these years. Steam engines, Cyrus McCormick's mechanical reaper, cook stoves, sewing machines, and a host of other labor-saving devices combined to make the old system based on slave labor an economic liability instead of a necessity, and slavery all but disappeared in Fairfax County's agriculture and industry.

Railroads and telegraph lines crossed the county; turnpike roads for all seasons were built; and canals connected the wharves and warehouses of Alexandria with the farms of the Shenandoah Valley and the mines of western Virginia. People traveled more widely and more easily than ever before. Political, social, and cultural patterns of attitudes and behavior were affected.

How the people of Fairfax County viewed these new developments in their technology, their society and economy, and in their political system could be the subject of extended study. Yet they saw it clearly enough to turn Fairfax County from the barren wasteland described by travelers through Northern Virginia prior to the 1830s into the "comparative Eden" described by visitors in the 1850s.

From the time of their first settlements, the Potomac River inspired Virginians to think of developing a waterway to the Ohio Valley. The upper and lower parts of the river were navigable, although when the water level was low in summer many miles of rocky bottoms were dangerous. But the Great Falls stood as an insurmountable barrier to connecting these two segments. The awesome power of this falls was increased by its sudden appearance to the traveler, as noted by John Davis, writing in 1805: "I now ascended a hill that led to the Great Falls and on a sudden my steps were suspended by the conflicts of elements, the strife of nature. I beheld the course of a large river abruptly obstructed by rocks over which it was breaking with a tremendous roar; while the foam of the water seemed ascending to the clouds, and the shores that confined it seemed to tremble at the convolutions." (Templeman and Netherton, Heritage). Drawing by G. Beck, Philadelphia; engraved by J. Cartwright, London, 1802

George Washington and his neighbors who were interested in developing western lands actively promoted the idea of constructing a canal around the Great Falls. In 1785 they organized the Patowmack Company to undertake this pioneering project. Work began on the locks at Great Falls in 1793 and by 1802 the entire series of canals and locks was substantially complete. President John Adams presided at the opening of the canal for navigation in 1802. Down the river, through the locks, and on to Georgetown and Alexandria came cargoes of furs, flour, whiskey, and lumber packed in flat-bottomed barges called gondolas. Courtesy of Fairfax County Library Photographic Archive

The importance of having a bridge across the Potomac at the Little Falls was recognized early, and in 1797 the first bridge at that point was built by the Georgetown Potomac Bridge Company. It was a covered wooden structure designed by Timothy Palmer of Newburyport, Massachusetts. A combination of weathering and heavy loads caused its collapse in 1804. Another one was immediately constructed, using wooden arches carried by a wooden truss, but within six months it was carried away. The original Chain Bridge, shown here, was the third bridge built at that site. It was designed so that its 128-foot deck of oak planks was suspended from chains made of four-and-a-half foot links anchored in massive stone abutments, based on a design patented by James Finley of Uniontown, Pennsylvania. This bridge lasted until 1852, and it was an essential link in the road system by which wagon transports and herds of animals moved from the Shenandoah Valley to the auction houses of Georgetown in the first half of the nineteenth century. Drawing about 1805; courtesy of United States Commission on Fine Arts

The Fairfax County Courthouse of 1800, shown here, was designed by James Wren who earlier had designed Pohick Church, The Falls Church, and Alexandria's Christ Church. The courthouse reflected an architectural style that originated in the arcaded market halls of Flanders and the Netherlands in the seventeenth century and was copied in a number of English town halls in the eighteenth century. In Virginia the style introduced by Fairfax County was copied in the courthouses of Nelson (1807), Caroline (1808), Sussex (1825), and Madison (1829) counties. Drawing by Gloria Matthews; courtesy of Fairfax County Office of Comprehensive Planning

*L*and speculation was great along the river in the vicinity of the Patowmack Company's canal in anticipation of wealth to be derived there. In 1790 the Virginia General Assembly issued a charter for the Town of Matildaville, named in honor of the wife of its founder, "Light Horse Harry" Lee. The town was located on forty acres at the Great Falls owned by Bryan Fairfax and served as the Patowmack Company's headquarters from 1785 to 1799. It consisted of a warehouse, forge, gristmill, sawmill, shops, barracks for laborers, a residence for the superintendent, and several boarding houses. The record of freight passing through the canal during the next eighteen years, shown in the table (left) as published by the Board of Public Works, fell short of expectations, and Matildaville failed to attract either population or wealth. The season when water was high enough for navigation on the river was about two months a year, and the cost of keeping the river clear of obstructions continually strained the company's resources. *Courtesy of Fairfax County Library Photographic Archive*

Table IV

A TABLE Shewing the amount of Tolls received by the Potomac Company in each year, from the 1st August, 1799, to the 1st August, 1817, together with the number of boats and tonnage employed, and the produce and merchandise transported, with the estimated value of the same during that period.

Years.	Boats.	Tonnage.	Flour.	Whiskey.	Tobacco.	Iron.	Articles of Produce Estimated.	Return Goods Estimated.	Amount of Tolls Received.	Total Estimated Value.
							Dolls. cts.	Dolls. cts.	Dolls. cts.	Dolls. cts.
1800	296	1,643	16,584	84	25		2,950	7,851 00	2,133 58	129,414 00
1801	413	2,993	28,209	619 1-2	100	187 1-2	14,060	6,180 00	4,210 19	328,445 32
2	305	1,952	17,250	379	5	238 1-2	27,233 50	000 00	3,479 63	163,916 00
3	493	5,549	45,065	257	32	480 1-2	3,936 00	10,386 00	9,353 93	345,472 82
4	426	3,823	39,350	578	8	88	3,250 00	7,514 00	7,665 58	284,040 60
5	405	3,208	28,507	436	11	137	32,975 18	7,486 00	5,213 24	340,334 18
6	203	1,226	19,079	459	5	20 1-2	3,553 40	4,998 00	2,123 69	86,790 40
7	573	8,155	85,248	971	20	35	11,796 00	7,314 00	15,080 42	551,896 47
8	508	5,994	48,463	1,535	3	13	10,532 47	7,613 00	9,924 27	337,007 47
9	603	6,767	40,039	1,527	37	494	8,537 00	11,510 00	9,094 89	305,628 00
10	568	5,374	40,757	1,080	13	191 1-2	5,703 00	000 00	7,915 85	318,237 62
11	1300	16,350	118,222	3,768	27	200	6,810 00	6,000 00	22,542 89	925,074 80
12	613	9,214	55,829	3,143	6	360	1,694 00	7,319 75	11,471 37	515,525 75
13	623	7,916	55,902	3,464	11	252	1,899 00	6,119 32	11,816 22	423,340 32
14	596	5,987	38,769	2,684	18	361	675 60	5,314 12	9,109 82	312,093 72
15	613	6,354	47,183	4,616	9	314	2,075 00	5,211 15	9,789 57	489,498 15
16	550	6,132	35,918	1,774	29	419	9,291 65	6,371 35	7,501 52	357,661 00
17	856	8,197	57,662	1,385	10	335	4,094 00	14,000 00	13,948 23	787,994 00
		106,834 1-2	818,026	28,759 1-2	369	4,126 1-2	151,065 80	121,187 69	162,379 95	7,002,370 62

True Statement from the Books.

JOS. BREWER, Tr. P. Co.

As federal officials evacuated Washington, the people of Alexandria on August 25, 1814, heard the news that British warships were in the Potomac. Wanting only to avoid having a battle fought in its vicinity, the city sent a delegation to the British commander asking for terms on which he would spare the port. The ransom was high, and for three days British crews loaded their squadron with the contents of Alexandria's warehouses. While this was under way, the city leaders sent a messenger to stop the American militia that was hurrying to their rescue, and asked them not to interfere with the capitulation. Finally, on September 2, the British left Alexandria, taking with them twenty-one confiscated vessels and merchandise valued at over $100,000. Later this incident was pictured in a cartoon titled "Johnny Bull and the Alexandrians." *Courtesy of Virginia State Library*

In the War of 1812, Fairfax County and Alexandria were the scenes of much excitement but little fighting. Generally Northern Virginians were not much concerned about the war until in 1814 British troops marched on Washington. The Tenth Virginia Militia, commanded by Colonel George Minor of Fairfax County, were mustered at Falls Church and ordered to assist in the defense of Washington. Confusion prevailed, however, and in the end all attention was focused on removing government records and military supplies to safety in Virginia. The Declaration of Independence and secret journals of Congress were packed in a linen bag and left hidden near Chain Bridge. The gunpowder at the Washington Navy Yard—150 barrels— was taken to the Dulaney farm near Falls Church where it was guarded by the militia. Nearby Wren's Tavern was filled with soldiers and government officials coming and going with no evident plan of action.

President James Madison, Dolley Madison, and several cabinet members fled to Fairfax County on August 24, 1814. Secretary of State James Monroe went directly to Wiley's Tavern near Great Falls. Secretary of the Navy

William Jones and Mrs. Madison headed toward Salona where it was arranged they would meet the President. Meanwhile, using another route, Madison and Attorney General Benjamin Rush stopped at Wren's before finally going on to Salona and Wiley's. Shown here, Salona today remains a stately mansion and grounds surrounded by the McLean community (Anderson, Salona). Courtesy of Fairfax County Library Photographic Archive

The War of 1812 and the embargoes that preceded it restricted foreign commerce and forced Americans to increase efforts to develop their own resources. This accelerated the demand for better transportation, which was sought through construction of toll roads, called turnpikes. Roads of major regional importance linked Alexandria to Leesburg (Route 7), to Aldie at the Little River (Route 236), and connected Leesburg to Georgetown via the Chain Bridge (Route 193). All these roads crossed Fairfax County and directly affected social and economic conditions. Most of these roads used the new roadbuilding technique of packed stones that recently had been developed in England by John McAdam. Roads of this type enabled local stage lines to offer regular service throughout the year in the 1820s and '30s. Courtesy of Library of Congress

Where it was practicable, the roads constructed by the turnpike companies in the early part of the nineteenth century used the methods developed by John McAdam in England. This method called for putting down layers of stones, rolling them, and shaping the top with a rounded crown to let water run off into the ditches instead of standing in the road. Where stone was not available for this method, however, a smooth surfaced road could be made by putting down layers of logs and planks covered with dirt. It is possible the technique of building plank roads came to Fairfax County from New York, the place of their first American success, brought by farmers migrating to Northern Virginia in the early 1840s. In 1851 the Virginia General Assembly authorized construction of two plank roads from Fairfax Court House, one running to the Orange and Alexandria Railroad near Fairfax Station, and the other to a point on the Potomac near Georgetown. Painting by Carl Rakeman; courtesy of Federal Highway Administration

From the time of Captain John Smith onward, reports of the abundant fish harvests of the Potomac and Chesapeake Bay excited the interest of those who settled Fairfax County. Fishing, both for subsistence and for export from Alexandria and Georgetown, was carried on widely. Shad and herring, caught each year in the spring, were the staples of this activity. The introduction of large seines up to more than 7,000 feet in length on the Potomac in the 1830s, however, drove many small fishermen out of business. Courtesy of Virginia State Library

As the rich lands of the Shenandoah Valley became linked by turnpikes to the ports of Alexandria, Georgetown, and Baltimore, and as farmers in Fairfax and Loudoun counties turned from tobacco to diversified crops, wheat and corn came to be important parts of the area's agricultural economy. This led to the rise of merchant milling along the most-traveled roads. Flour was easier to haul than bags of grain and commanded a higher price in the seaport cities, so many farmers had their grain ground into flour at these mills. The mill at Colvin Run, shown here, is typical of the mills that served both the local neighborhood needs and the merchant trade. Built about 1811, possibly on the site of an earlier smaller structure, this mill was rebuilt in the 1960s by the Fairfax County Park Authority. Today it offers the visitor a chance to step back into the life of the early 1800s. Jack Hiller photo

Hope Park Mill is typical of the mills that served local needs from colonial times through the nineteenth century. Its date of construction is uncertain, but was probably between 1790 and 1804 when Hope Park plantation was owned by Dr. David Stuart, who served in the Virginia House of Delegates and as the first Virginia Commissioner for the District of Columbia. Stuart shared many interests with George Washington, which led to an extensive correspondence between them, and he was married to Martha Washington's widowed daughter-in-law, Eleanor Calvert Custis. Following Dr. Stuart's death in 1814 the mill passed through several other owners during the remainder of the nineteenth century, all of whom kept the mill operating as a grist mill serving local farmers' needs. In the 1890s and early 1900s, under the ownership of Major Frank Robey, who renamed it Robey's Mill, the old wooden grist mill enjoyed a remarkable period of prosperity. It was operated until the 1930s. Today this privately owned structure provides a rare view of an eighteenth century wooden grist mill and its outbuildings (Petersilia and Wright, Hope Park). Courtesy of Library of Congress

In colonial times and the years of growth in the early nineteenth century, the grist mill represented the high point of mechanical development and engineering skill. The massive interconnected system of gears, traveling belts, and sifting bins could be operated almost automatically with the power provided by a huge waterwheel which was balanced so perfectly that it could be turned by the flow of a cupful of water. The master millwright who designed and installed a mill was honored only slightly more than the master miller who presided over its daily operations and kept it in working order. Much of the Colvin Run Mill's gears and other machinery, shown here, were handmade from designs developed by Oliver Evans, the leading millwright-engineer of the early nineteenth century, whose designs were widely copied in Northern Virginia. Marcia Fram photo; courtesy of Fairfax County Library Photographic Archive

In the 1820s and '30s turnpike roads and regular coaching schedules led to increased passenger travel and brought the heyday of the wayside inn. Many of these establishments traced their origin to "ordinaries" of colonial times, and continued the practice of offering guests the ordinary fare of the proprietor's household in accordance with its daily schedule. The Dranesville Tavern, standing beside the Alexandria-Leesburg Turnpike (Route 7), pictured here as it appears today (right), invites the visitor to return to a time, a century earlier, when it was described by the Alexandria Gazette as "one of the best roadside inns in the state of Virginia."

This tavern, which was rehabilitated by the Fairfax County Park Authority in the 1970s, originally was constructed in 1823 as a pair of log cabins connected by enclosing a breezeway between them. In the 1850s the entire structure was covered with clapboards and an addition was made to house a kitchen and upstairs room. The tavern at Dranesville served all who traveled the turnpike—the driver and passengers of the mail coach, the wagoner and his team, and the drover moving to market at the plodding pace of his animals. Accordingly, the tavern building was surrounded with sheds and pens where the animals could be fed, watered, and kept safe overnight. During the later years of the nineteenth century and early twentieth century, the innkeeper operated a small general merchandise store in a separate building.

The tavern that stands at Dranesville today is the survivor of several that were in that vicinity during the turnpike days. The sites of six have been identified and documented in varying degrees. Dranesville was about fifteen miles from Alexandria and Georgetown—about a day's walk for a drover and his herd, or a half-way point between Alexandria and Leesburg—and a customary stopping place in a day's journey. For the most part in their day such taverns were known by the names of their proprietors —Jackson, Jenkins, Farr, Washington Drane—and they often functioned as the post office, school, and neighborhood meeting place.

In 1968 when the Leesburg Pike was widened, the Dranesville Tavern was moved to its present site and rehabilitated by the Fairfax County Park Authority. Its removal required stripping away some of the siding and showed its original construction as two log houses connected by an enclosed breezeway. Some details of this contruction can be seen in the photograph below. Photo of restored tavern by Richard Netherton; photo of tavern about to be renovated, by Bernie Boston

If news of the successful trip of the locomotive Tom Thumb from Baltimore in 1830 did not alarm the merchants of Alexandria, the report five years later that the Baltimore and Ohio Railroad was opening service between Baltimore and Washington should have done so. At that time Alexandria was a thriving seaport where sometimes ships lined up all the way to the Chesapeake Bay waiting for space at the city's docks. Competition between Alexandria and Baltimore was keen. Up to that time the commerce of both ports was fed by a system of inland turnpikes reaching west and south. Wagons moved at a pace of three miles an hour when they were not mired in mud or making roadside repairs. Trains traveling on smooth rails at twenty miles an hour could give their users a commanding advantage in competition for trade.

Alarm turned to panic in 1842 when Alexandrians heard that the Winchester and Potomac Railroad had finished spiking a feeder route to the B&O's main line at Harper's Ferry. Alexandria had put its reliance on the Chesapeake and Ohio Canal, begun in 1828, to bring to it the farm products of the Shenandoah Valley and the coal of Wheeling.

It seemed clear that this race would be lost to Baltimore unless rails could promptly be laid across Northern Virginia. Even so Alexandria did not move until 1847 when a group of local merchants obtained a charter for the Alexandria and Harper's Ferry Railroad, only to have it dissolve without laying a foot of rail. Six years passed before another attempt was made, this time under the name of Alexandria, Loudoun and Hampshire Railroad. By the summer of 1859, this line was hauling freight and passengers as far as Herndon; in May 1860 service to Leesburg was inaugurated.

Another railroad venture, also chartered in 1847, made steady progress in the decade that followed and eventually linked Alexandria with Gordonsville in central Virginia. The line of the Orange and Alexandria Railroad reached southwest from Alexandria, encouraging the growth of new communities at the stations of Seminary, Edsall's, Springfield, Ravensworth, Burke's, Sideburn, Fairfax Station, and Clifton (Williams, W&OD; Harwood, Rails; Netherton, Clifton). Drawing by Robert Clay; courtesy of Virginia State Library

Regardless of the seriousness of the issues that demanded consideration, politics in Virginia in the 1850s remained, as it always had been, a social as well as civic activity. Barbecues at political rallies were among the favorite activities of Virginians, and the drawing shown here depicts the elaborate preparation for such an occasion in which pigs were roasted over a trough filled with burning charcoal and continually basted with sauce by cooks with long-handled brooms. Courtesy of Virginia Historical Society

In an effort to encourage manufacturing industries, merino sheep were introduced into Northern Virginia to provide the basis for a woolen industry. George Washington Parke Custis was a strong advocate of this activity. This silver trophy was awarded to William Foote of Hayfield, a magistrate of the Fairfax County Court in April 1809 at one of the annual sheep shearing contests held by George Washington Parke Custis of Arlington House. Courtesy of George Washington Bicentennial Center, Alexandria

*A*nother change set in motion by the economic growth of the early nineteenth century resulted in a restructuring of the county government. In 1850 the Fairfax County Court was composed of men of the county's leading landed families, elected by a relatively small proportion of freeholders who could meet the election law's property requirements, which had changed very little since colonial times. The county court was thus almost a self-perpetuating body whose responsiveness to the new economic interests of the county was questioned. In 1850-51 a new state constitution was drafted which opened up the suffrage to all white males over twenty-one years of age who had lived in the county more than two years. In May 1852 the counties held their first elections under this new constitution, and a number of new members representing new interests were elected to the court.

Silas Burke was one who had taken an active part in the economic growth that ushered in this change. He had been an officer of the Fairfax Turnpike, and was a state director of the Orange and Alexandria Railroad. Burke Station was located on land which he sold to the railroad. Earlier he had organized one of the most successful agricultural clubs in Northern Virginia and worked to increase local acceptance of the principles of scientific farming demonstrated on his own extensive landholdings in Fairfax

County. Prior to 1850 he had served as presiding judge of the county court and advocated more progressive policies to aid growth. In the election of 1852 under the new constitution, he was again elected presiding judge and went on to serve with the respect and confidence of the public. His obituary, shown here, was spread on

the pages of the Fairfax County Court Minute Book framed in black, and to the present time it is the only instance of such a distinction being given by the court. Today his name is also perpetuated in the thriving Burke community in central Fairfax County. Courtesy of Fairfax County Court Clerk

Thomas ap Catesby Jones, shown here, was a naval hero in the War of 1812. Later he inherited Sharon, an "utterly barren and unproductive" estate near the Great Falls of the Potomac. It was a time when some said that "the more Fairfax land a man had, the poorer he was." But the challenge intrigued Jones, and he experimented with deep plowing and the use of lime and manures. From a naval expedition to South America in the 1820s, he returned with a quantity of guano, which he found made a particularly good fertilizer. Jones' progressive farming methods were noticed in both the South and North and attracted some in the North to think seriously about moving to Northern Virginia. Courtesy of Virginia State Library

The far-reaching changes that occurred in Fairfax County's economic conditions in the first half of the nineteenth century were reflected in equally striking changes in the social structure. As the large plantation-style landholdings, with their dependence on tobacco, were broken up and replaced by smaller family farms producing diversified crops, the need for a large slave population ceased. Although Alexandria continued to be a major slave market, the permanent slave population of the county steadily declined. At the same time the number of free blacks increased and, with special permission to do so, stayed on in the county as exceptions to the state law requiring freed slaves to leave.

Most freed blacks continued to do the work they always had, except that now they hired themselves by the day to landowners and shopkeepers. With the aid of friends such as the Fairfax

Quakers, however, some were able to obtain educations for themselves and their children and improve their economic and

social positions. One such black was West Ford, shown here as a young man. A former slave at Mount Vernon, he was freed and eventually became owner of the land on which the Gum Springs community is now located. He was widely known and respected, and one reported incident suggests the reason for it: when Harper's Magazine ran an article on Mount Vernon in 1859, the artist-reporter talked to Ford, then seventy-one years old, about his childhood as a slave in the Washington family. Ford agreed to sit next day for a sketch. When the artist arrived he found Ford prepared wearing "a black satin vest, a silk cravat, and his curly grey hair arranged in the best manner. 'For,' he said, 'the artists make colored people look bad enough anyhow.'" (Hickin, Fairfax County). Original charcoal drawing of West Ford as a handsome young man owned by Henry S. Robinson; courtesy of Fairfax County Library Photographic Archive

On June 17, 1861, a railroad was used tactically for the first time in warfare during the Civil War. On that day four companies of the First Ohio Volunteer Regiment, riding in cars of the Alexandria, Loudoun and Hampshire Railroad, were fired on as they approached Vienna. Seeing the superior forces of the Confederates facing them, the Union troops scattered in the woods and were stranded as the frightened engineers ran their locomotives backward to Alexandria. This picture is a newspaper artist's recreation of the scene for Frank Leslie's Illustrated Weekly *(Fairfax County Civil War Centennial Commission). Courtesy of Falls Church Public Library*

5

The Years of War: 1861-1865

The years from 1861 to 1865 had a particularly deep impact on Fairfax County. At the outset the county's residents were strongly divided in their sentiments on union and secession, and this continued until the end. It was reflected in the constant presence of armies either camping or campaigning. Only one major engagement was fought in Fairfax County—when, after the Second Battle of Manassas, Lee sent Jackson to test the strength of the retreating Federal forces—and yet for four years residents of the county lived in disputed territory where any day or night could bring fresh alarms. In hundreds of skirmishes, now recalled only by the name of a Marr or a Mosby—one a casualty almost at the outset and the other so indestructible as to become a living legend—the war left its mark almost daily.

The effect of being at the gateway of Washington and in the corridor to Richmond can only be imagined today. Yet to those who lived here in 1861-65, it brought real and profound changes. Fairfax County was the first to be invaded and occupied by military forces. Daily life was immediately disrupted. Personal travel and transport of goods were possible only by passes from the army currently occupying the area. Even if crops in the field survived foraging parties or were not trampled underfoot by troops on the move, it was always uncertain whether their owner could keep a wagon and horse or mule or ox to haul them to market. Business of any kind was carried on only with the greatest difficulty.

The appetite of the armies for timber was unbelievable. Wooded hillsides for miles were cut clear of trees to get lumber for the defenses of Washington, and the Confederate forts and hutments at Centreville. And, when military action interrupted the rail and canal connection with the coal mines of West Virginia, the Union army sent a corps of woodcutters into the field to assure a supply of firewood for the U.S. Military Railroad system. These were losses that could not be restored. Only slightly less costly was the destruction of bridges, railroads, mills, and public facilities, and the long-term damage to farmland and orchards.

Against this background there were many instances in which the human spirit prevailed against the hardships brought by the war. Clara Barton's ceaseless efforts to get aid and better medical care for the wounded, and her own example as a nurse, have been deservedly remembered. But many other examples were not honored, or even recognized, at the time. Such were the cases of the heroic women who refused to leave their homes when the fighting started, and whose presence was the factor that often saved their homes from destruction.

Other acts were noted at the time and credited with shaping the course of the war. McClellan's

achievement was taking the raw recruits of the North and, in a few months after Bull Run, turning them into the Army of the Potomac with pride in themselves and confidence in their leaders. Also noteworthy, in the later years of the war, was the loyalty of the Southern partisans who fought on in Fairfax County, in the heart of the enemy's stronghold.

Still other examples of heroism in the human spirit dealt with hopes that could not be immediately fulfilled. Among those were the hopes of thousands of blacks who came as refugees to freedom behind Union lines and endured untold hardships so their children could be free and receive an education. Also ahead of their time were the ideas for liberal reconstruction and economic development which Francis Pierpont, the Governor of "loyal" Virginia, and some of his Fairfax County advisors proposed for the postwar era.

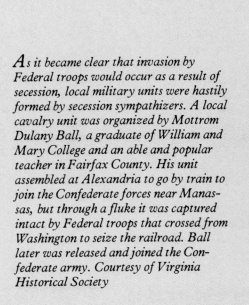

As it became clear that invasion by Federal troops would occur as a result of secession, local military units were hastily formed by secession sympathizers. A local cavalry unit was organized by Mottrom Dulany Ball, a graduate of William and Mary College and an able and popular teacher in Fairfax County. His unit assembled at Alexandria to go by train to join the Confederate forces near Manassas, but through a fluke it was captured intact by Federal troops that crossed from Washington to seize the railroad. Ball later was released and joined the Confederate army. Courtesy of Virginia Historical Society

Within days after Virginia seceded, Union troops occupied strategic hills and crossroads in Fairfax County to protect the city of Washington. Eventually an extensive system of fortifications was built along a large arc stretching from south of Alexandria up to Chain Bridge. In the summer of 1861 the crossroads community of Falls Church marked the outer rim of the territory occupied by the Union defenders. Shown here are Union cavalry pickets at The Falls Church. Courtesy of Falls Church Historical Commission

As Union troops occupied Alexandria and the northern part of Fairfax County, and Confederate units formed in the western and southern parts, civilian life was a victim of the confusion and speed with which events moved. Outside the areas guarded by Federal troops, pockets of Union sympathizers were harassed by secessionists and driven from their homes. In areas occupied by the Federals, civilians suspected of secession political activity or spying were arrested. The drawing above from Harper's Weekly *shows "the Misses Scott" and their father being escorted to prison in Washington and illustrates the fate of many civilians suspected of rebel activity (Steadman, Falls Church). Courtesy of Melvin L. Steadman*

The crisis of secession found public opinion in Fairfax County badly divided. Most were opposed to the radical tactics of John Brown and favored conciliation with the abolitionists to avoid secession. The county's delegate to the secession convention in Richmond was a moderate. Despite the convention's results, Fairfax County remained badly split with several pockets of anti-secession feeling where Northerners had settled. When the popular referendum on secession was held in May 1861, however, the vote favoring it was one-sided, 1,231 to 289. Lincoln's call for troops to invade Virginia swung some undecided voters to favor secession, but a cartoon from Harper's Weekly emphasizes the pressure that was put on voters by the secessionists. Courtesy of Virginia State Library

HOW VIRGINIA WAS VOTED OUT OF THE UNION.

Gov. William ("Extra Billy") Smith

Capt. John Quincy Marr

As Confederate units gathered throughout Northern Virginia and their presence threatened Washington, the Federal troops harassed them with raids and sorties. On June 1, 1861, a Confederate unit camped at Fairfax Court House was caught off guard by a Union cavalry patrol which routed it with a colorful charge through the village. Captain John Quincy Marr became the first Confederate officer killed in action in the war. Among the Confederates involved in this incident was the former Governor, William "Extra Billy" Smith. Courtesy of Civil War Centennial Commission

62

Union political leaders, hoping that a major military victory over the Confederate forces would stop the secession movement, put pressure on General Irvin McDowell, commander of the Federal troops in Washington, to take the initiative and strike the Confederate forces gathered near Manassas and marauding throughout Fairfax County. McDowell gathered 35,000 men from the freshly recruited units that had come to Washington from the North, and marched out. This drawing shows a column of wagons crossing the old Pimmit Run Bridge and moving up Chain Bridge Hill. This terrain has changed little in the past century and the stone abutments of the bridge can be seen today. Courtesy of Eleanor Lee Templeman and Arlington County Library

As McDowell's army of 35,000 men moved on the road through Fairfax Court House and Centreville, Beauregard withdrew his force of 22,000 men behind Bull Run and waited. By coordinating his own movements with General Joseph Johnston's force in the Shenandoah Valley, the Confederate commander hoped he could slip in between McDowell's army and its rear base, defeat it, and then overrun the Union outposts at Fairfax Court House and Falls Church, not stopping until Alexandria was occupied. This plan was thwarted, however, when, on July 21, 1861, Union troops seized the initiative by crossing Bull Run and outflanking the Confederate line.

Although the Confederate line was forced back dangerously by the Union attack, it held until part of Johnston's army from the valley arrived by train and enabled it to counterattack. Suffering from poor coordination of its units, the Union lines broke and began a confused retreat. The Union defeat was complete and McDowell's troops did not stop until next day when they reached the defenses of Washington (Jones, First Manassas). Courtesy of Fairfax County Library Photographic Archive

A Confederate Bull Battery

Although victorious at Bull Run, the Confederates were too exhausted and inadequately equipped to take the offensive beyond reoccupying the southern and western parts of Fairfax County. Meanwhile the Union forces hastened work on the fortifications of Washington in the northern part of the county. In this defense plan it was vitally important to keep the railroads operating so they could be used when the Union army resumed the offensive. One strategic point in the rail network was Union Mills, near present-day Clifton. This photograph shows Union Mills on the Orange and Alexandria Railroad. Courtesy of Library of Congress

While regiments from the northern states arrived in Washington by train in response to President Lincoln's call for volunteers, one Confederate army gathered near Manassas under the command of General P. G. T. Beauregard and another gathered in the Shenandoah Valley under General Joseph Johnston. Assembly of the Confederate units was slowed because of the lack of railroads in many parts of the South. Supplies and equipment moved by whatever means was available, and, although it was not usual for oxen to haul artillery pieces, this drawing by a Confederate soldier shows that it may sometimes have been necessary. Courtesy of Fairfax County Library Photographic Archive

The rolling hills of the Bull Run battlefield today are preserved as a national historic shrine. Its statues of generals and markers of military units look out upon a farm scene that has changed very little from the 1860s. Jane Robinson photo; courtesy of Fairfax County Library Photographic Archive

THE GREAT REVIEW AT BAILEY'S CROSS ROADS, VIRGINIA, ON NOVEMBER 20, 1861.—SKETCHED BY OUR SPECIAL ARTIST FROM THE TOP OF A BARN.—[SEE PAGE 772.]

During the summer and fall of 1861, McClellan organized, trained, and drilled the new Army of the Potomac. Parades and inspections were held regularly, and led one Pennsylvanian to write home: "When the Major or Brigadier General are favored with the visits of some particular friends of course a big parade must be held. This is as necessary as dessert is to a dinner. 'It is fine fun for the boys, but death to the frogs,' as Mr. Aesop would say."

The Grand Review held in November

1861 exceeded all others. That day in the fields between Munson's Hill and Bailey's Crossroads approximately 100,000 men passed in review for McClellan, President Lincoln, and other distinguished visitors from Washington. Later one enlisted man from Massachusetts declared: "This is a day long to be remembered by thousands of people as one of the most eventful in their lives. Never before in this country has there been assembled together such an immense body of armed men as were reviewed today on

the 'sacred soil' of Virginia."

These parades, as well as the other training, gave the new soldiers and officers a chance to assess each other's qualities, sort out the misfits, and develop an esprit de corps that had been missing before. There also were opportunities for small units to patrol and probe the strength of the nearby Confederate outposts and generally to become familiar with the field soldier's life (Cooling, Symbol). Courtesy of Virginia State Library

The recruits, fresh from the farms of Vermont, Michigan, and Wisconsin, who made up the new Army of the Potomac never had seen a sight such as Professor Thaddeus Lowe's observation balloon. Yet it became a frequent topic of comment in the summer and fall of 1861 as it soared serenely over the defenses of Washington watching the roads to Centreville for telltale signs of Confederate troops on the move or directing Union artillery fire in the outpost areas around Falls Church, Vienna, and Bailey's Crossroads (Cooling, Symbol). Courtesy of Virginia State Library

After their victory at Bull Run, the Confederate forces watched and waited in the area between Manassas and Fairfax Court House, with advance outposts at Munson's Hill and Minor's Hill. General Beauregard established his headquarters at Fairfax Court House, and here, in October 1861, there occurred a conference that turned out to be of the greatest importance to the Southern cause. Here Generals Johnston, Beauregard, and Smith met with President Jefferson Davis to consider a plan to gather all available troops and strike at Washington before McClellan's new Army of the Potomac was ready. Davis, however, was keenly aware that leaders in the Southern states and Congress were unwilling to send troops away from their home bases, and would not approve the plan. As a result a stalemate was created and Johnston ordered his army back to Centreville for the winter. This photograph of the Fairfax courthouse shows Union troops who quickly moved into the former Confederate outpost (Cooling, Bull Run). T. H. O'Sullivan photo; courtesy of Library of Congress

Fear that McClellan would move the new Union army against them in the spring prompted the Confederate officers to fortify their base at Centreville. Once this work began, the idle army was kept busy digging and building. The result was a system of fortifications that was not surpassed until World War I and, later, the Maginot Line. Because the existing road connecting Centreville with Manassas was wholly inadequate to carry the supplies needed for this work, a special spur railroad line was constructed from the Orange and Alexandria Railroad's tracks at Manassas. It was named The Centreville Military Railroad and was the first of its kind in the world. Despite this railroad connection, it was impossible to obtain all the supplies and equipment needed at Centreville. Accordingly some of the artillery ports were mounted with Quaker guns—logs set in positions to deceive enemy observers into thinking that genuine guns were in place. This photograph shows a corner of the vast earthworks as the Union troops found them when they entered the abandoned forts a year later (Cooling, Bull Run). Courtesy of Library of Congress

At Centreville, the Confederate leaders faced the problems of providing winter housing for 40,000 men and constructing warehouses, kitchens, and fortifications. When the promise of ten portable saw-mills from Richmond did not materialize, the soldiers resorted to hand-hewn log construction, leveling every tree for miles around. Later observers cited this as the beginning of the destruction that left large parts of Fairfax and Prince William counties as barren as deserts by the end of the war. The cabins displayed a wide variety of styles and construction, yet they enabled the Confederate army in Northern Virginia to survive the harsh winter of 1861-62 despite a high rate of casualties due to disease (Cooling, Bull Run). Courtesy of Brady Collection, Library of Congress

By the summer of 1861 the civilians who remained in Fairfax County began to feel the effects of having opposing armies quartered in their vicinity. Normally, the things that the armies of both sides needed were brought to them in wagon trains that moved in long lines behind the columns of marching men. Occasionally, however, some of the soldiers' food moved on the hoof. Thus the much-maligned diet of salted meat, hardtack, coffee, dried beans, and other things that could be boxed, crated, or barreled was varied with a taste of fresh beef. When camps were set up in the field, cooks would slaughter animals from the herds and distribute the meat to the units' quartermasters. It was still further divided until it came to the portions for the small groups of six to eight men who did their own cooking. Shown here is a rare eye-witness sketch of cattle being swum across Occoquan River on their way to troops in Fairfax County (Stern, Soldier Life). From Harper's Weekly; courtesy of Virginia State Library

The flow of supplies always was unpredictable, and armies of both sides regularly foraged for food in the country-side, often by authority of the army commander. This drawing depicts an incident reported to have occurred in the vicinity of Annandale as a Union foraging party overtook a group of farmers' wagons with farm produce on its way to the markets in Alexandria or Washington. A decade after the war was over, loyal residents of Fairfax County whose personal property had been seized by Union troops on orders from their officers were able to recover some compensation from the Federal government for their losses. Their accounts are in the National Archives in Washington. Courtesy of Virginia State Library

In March 1862, at a council of corps commanders held at Fairfax Court House, McClellan unfolded his plan to shift the bulk of the Union army by ships to the peninsula between the James and York Rivers and there march directly up to Richmond. As this campaign began, Johnston and Beauregard moved their armies to the defense of the Confederate capital, leaving behind the empty buildings and earthworks around Centreville. Mathew Brady's photograph of Centreville in the spring of 1862 looks up Braddock Road past the Methodist Church and reveals the destitute condition of the town after the Confederate occupation. Courtesy of Fairfax County Library Photographic Archive

When McClellan stalled in his march up the peninsula to Richmond, Lincoln appointed Major General John Pope to the command of a new Army of Virginia, consisting of the Federal troops in the Washington area, and ordered him to take the offensive. Pope moved toward Manassas, but the Confederates, now commanded by Lee, drew the Union army into a trap, defeated it soundly, and sent it retreating back into Fairfax County and the defenses of Washington. Lee sent Jackson to smash the retreating Union forces, but he was stopped at Chantilly (Ox Hill), in the western part of Fairfax County, by Union troops under General Kearney (Cooling, Bull Run; Smith, Centreville). Courtesy of Virginia State Library

Brig. General Isaac Stevens

Maj. General Philip Kearny

*T*he Battle of Chantilly (or Ox Hill, as Confederate records refer to it) was fought on September 1, 1862, the only major battle fought in Fairfax County during the war. Popular accounts highlighted its hand-to-hand fighting during a blinding rainstorm and the death in action of two Union Generals, Major General Philip Kearney and Brigadier General Isaac Stevens. But historians see it as convincing Lee that he could not attack the City of Washington directly and that he must invade the North by the road to Antietam (Cooling, Symbol). On the site of the Battle of Chantilly today may be seen two stone markers commemorating the deaths of Kearney and Stevens. Courtesy of Fairfax County Civil War Centennial Commission

*W*hen the casualties of the Second Battle of Manassas were brought off the field, many were left at Fairfax Station to wait for transportation to hospitals in Alexandria and Washington. They lay in St. Mary's Church or on the hillside under the trees. Among those who nursed them was Clara Barton, a clerk in the Patent Office and the first woman to hold such a position. She had no official connection with the army and had come out from the City of Washington solely because of her concern for the suffering of the wounded. Her activity in nursing and bringing supplies to the soldiers in the field attracted nationwide attention and support. Eventually it led to the founding of the American Red Cross. Courtesy of Virginia State Library

*S*t. Mary's Church at Fairfax Station stands today as a lovely country Roman Catholic Church which serves both as a house of worship and a symbol of universal humanity. Built in 1858 by Irish immigrants who had come to Northern Virginia to work on the Orange and Alexandria Railroad, it became the site of Clara Barton's work to help the wounded soldiers from the Second Battle of Manassas. There is a local legend that when General U. S. Grant was president he heard that Union soldiers once had used the church pews for firewood and immediately furnished new ones which still are in use (Rodrigues, St. Mary's). Painting by Gerald Hennesy, used with permission of the artist

71

After Lee's invasion of the North ended at Antietam, the military action in the winter of 1862 and spring of 1863 shifted south of the Rappahannock River. Fairfax County enjoyed a quiet period in which no major campaigning was carried on in its vicinity. For the Union troops occupying Northern Virginia, the most important thing was to keep the transportation system working so that troops and supplies could move to the fighting fronts. Streams where bridges had been destroyed often were crossed on pontoon bridges. The bridge at Blackburn's Ford, near Centreville, pictured here, was typical of many built by the Union army to ease the problem of transportation. Courtesy of Brady Collection, National Archives

Early in the war a loyal government was organized at Wheeling, in northwestern Virginia, and elected a "Restored" General Assembly, with Francis Harrison Pierpont as Acting Governor. Unionists in Fairfax County and Alexandria worked with this government to create a local organization that could meet civilian needs. A Fairfax County Court met at the Village of West End (Alexandria) in a building that before the war had belonged to one of the county's largest slave traders.

When West Virginia entered the Union in 1863, Pierpont and his loyalist government moved to Alexandria. Several Fairfax County Unionists became close advisors to Pierpont and supported his proposals for a liberal reconstruction program of education, economic reconstruction, and voting reform. Courtesy of Virginia State Library

Early in the war the Federal government organized the U.S. Military Railroads Commission to coordinate and expedite use of the railroads, particularly in occupied areas. It built new lines and seized and operated captured tracks and trains in the South. One of the most able and energetic officials of this organization was Brigadier General Herman

Haupt. Largely because of his untiring work, it became possible for trains on the Baltimore and Ohio tracks to go through Washington, across the Potomac to Alexandria, and on to the armies in the field over the tracks of the Orange and Alexandria or the Alexandria, Loudoun and Hampshire railroads. Catching his willingness to become personally involved,

a Brady photograph shows him in 1865 (standing on the bank in a long black coat), supervising construction of a siding at Devereux Station (later Clifton) on the Orange and Alexandria Railroad (Williams, W&OD; Cooling, Symbol). Courtesy of Brady Collection, Library of Congress

Lewis McKenzie was the first president of the Alexandria, Loudoun and Hampshire Railroad, and one of Alexandria's most successful businessmen. In contrast to many of his friends, he was a staunch Unionist. On the morning that Federal troops occupied Northern Virginia he flew American flags on his locomotives, but this did not save the railroad from military seizure or hasten its return to McKenzie after the war. The government seizure of the AL&H lasted longer than for any other railroad in Virginia, and left it in badly damaged condition. Never-

theless, McKenzie energetically led the task of rebuilding it, and by June 1867 daily service between Alexandria and Leesburg was resumed to the great benefit of the entire region. During and after the war, McKenzie served in Congress, representing Northern Virginia, and held office as councilman and mayor of Alexandria, actively supporting a wide range of civic and charitable causes (Williams, W&OD). Portrait of McKenzie as a young man courtesy of Ames Williams

While General Herman Haupt was working to keep the military railroads operating, Colonel John S. Mosby was earning a reputation for tearing up Union railroads and ambushing supply columns and depots. Fairfax County became the site of this contest during 1863 and 1864.

Mosby had been a problem for the regular Confederate army during the early days of his enlistment from Abingdon, Virginia. But when allowed to organize his own irregular cavalry unit, he began a colorful and successful career in Northern Virginia. From early 1863 to the end of the war, he furnished General J. E. B. Stuart with supplies, wagons, and horses and mules taken from Union depots in Fairfax County, and furnished information about Union troop movements in Fairfax and Loudoun counties. This photograph was posed for Mathew Brady. Courtesy of Virgina State Library

One of Mosby's most celebrated exploits occurred on the night of March 9, 1863, in Fairfax Court House. There the Union Brigadier General Edwin Stoughton, Deputy Commander of the defenses of Washington, had made his headquarters in the comfortable brick house of Dr. William Gunnell near the center of town. On this chilly Sunday night shortly after falling asleep, Stoughton suddenly was jolted awake by a sharp slap on his bare rear. Stoughton, a lover of wine and women who had spent the evening enjoying both, was none too alert. "General," asked a slim figure above him, "did you ever hear of Mosby?" "Yes, have you caught him?" was the reply. "No," the visitor said, "but he has caught you." Minutes later, Stoughton with two Union captains, thirty privates, and fifty-eight horses were led off into the darkness by Mosby and his men. Next morning when President Lincoln heard of the affair, he complained that he would have no trouble making another General, but he sincerely regretted losing the horses. From the Rust Collection; courtesy of Fairfax County Library Photographic Archive*

Mosby's success in avoiding capture, despite a massive effort by Union commanders to catch him, was due partly to his having a series of hideouts in Loudoun County just out of reach of the garrisons defending Washington, and partly to having Southern sympathizers in Fairfax County on whom he could count to give him warnings and information.

Like many Virginia women, pretty nineteen-year-old Antonia Ford of Fairfax Court House enthusiastically supported the Confederate cause. She was so effective in supplying Stuart with information about Union troops in her neighborhood that he gave her a "commission" as a Major and named her his honorary aide-de-camp. This cartoon from Harper's Weekly satirized the whole affair. Antonia Ford was imprisoned in Washington for a time after one of Mosby's most daring raids, but eventually she married a Union officer, Joseph Willard. Courtesy of Virginia State Library*

During the latter part of the war, the civilian population experienced tragedy everywhere, but nowhere was it more striking than in the case of the blacks who sought refuge behind Union lines. After the Emancipation Proclamation declared that all slaves who escaped to Union-occupied territory were free, hundreds who had nothing to hold them on the land of their owners took to the roads as refugees. This drawing shows a family group that was fortunate enough to find a wagon and animals to draw it.

The Union-occupied areas of Fairfax County were the objective of many of these wanderers, but here they found the
Federal military and civil authorities unprepared to feed and house them or find them work. Around Alexandria, Falls Church, and present-day Arlington there grew up several new Freedmen's Villages. Generally, these were merely collections of shanties with none of the conveniences needed for health and safety. Work was scarce except for occasional day labor around the forts or railroads, or as household servants. All too often the freedman found his new living conditions more deplorable than those he had left. Courtesy of Virginia State Library

While their plight was less noticed than that of the wandering blacks, the problems facing many women who stayed on their land after all their menfolk were gone were also very critical. Anna Maria Fitzhugh of Ravensworth, the widow of an uncle of Mrs. Robert E. Lee, was the largest landowner in Fairfax County. She had managed her land and farms before the war, and despite her advancing age she insisted on remaining at Ravensworth after the fighting started. She was granted protection by the Union commanders who occupied Fairfax County and, unlike that of many of her neighbors, her property suffered little damage. When she died in 1874, Ravensworth was inherited by Mrs. Lee and her heirs.

The presence of women who were determined to preserve their homes and farms was the decisive factor in saving many notable places in Fairfax County from destruction during the war. George Washington's estate at Mount Vernon was spared in this way by the perseverance of Sarah Tracy, and Sully plantation was preserved by Maria Barlow who at times had to fight fires in the farm buildings left in the wake of foraging parties from both sides. Portrait of Anna Maria Fitzhugh as a young woman by Thomas Sully; courtesy of Virginia State Library

Because of its isolated location, the Chain Bridge was especially vulnerable. Throughout the war the national capital trembled with rumors of quick thrusts by the Confederates to capture it so that Lee could slip across the Potomac and into Washington by the back door. Equally serious would have been the destruction of the bridge by raiders. On the Virginia side of the river the bridge was guarded by Fort Marcy and Fort Ethan Allen,
built in the wooded high ground over-looking the Georgetown-Leesburg Turn-pike. This picture, probably drawn by one of the New York Volunteers who served there, shows the garrison's tents spread out around the small earthwork fort. Today a replica of Fort Marcy has been reconstructed on its original site by the National Park Service (Cooling, Symbol). Courtesy of Eleanor Lee Templeman

General Robert E. Lee, gathering his forces together in western Fairfax County after defeating the Union army at the Second Battle of Bull Run, seized the opportunity to launch the Confederacy's first invasion of the North. From the vicinity of Fairfax Court House, his force of 55,000 men moved along the Ox Road to Dranesville, and then to Leesburg and White's Ferry where he crossed the Potomac River into Maryland on September 5 and 6, 1862. Eleven days later, this invasion ended at Antietam in the bloodiest day of the Civil War. Historical markers posted near Fairfax (one-half mile west) and at Dranesville trace Lee's march through Fairfax County (Markers). Courtesy of Fairfax County Library Photographic Archive

Following the First Battle of Bull Run, Thomas Jonathan "Stonewall" Jackson encamped his brigade one mile outside Centreville and remained there throughout the summer of 1861 to block the way of any Union forces that might try to return along that route to invade Virginia.

A year later, after Lee's victory at the Second Battle of Bull Run, Jackson returned to Fairfax County in pursuit of General Pope's retreating Union army. At Chantilly (Ox Hill) the Federal troops turned and fought, sending Jackson back toward the Shenandoah Valley. Jackson photograph from J. B. Leib Photo Co., York, Pa.

Major General Pierre G. T. Beauregard, Confederate commander at the First Battle of Bull Run whose headquarters at Fairfax Court House later was the scene of Jefferson Davis' conference that decided not to invade the North

General Joseph E. Johnston, whose timely movement of troops from the Shenandoah Valley saved the Confederate fortunes at the First Battle of Bull Run and whose troops built the earthworks at Centreville in the fall of 1861

Major General J. E. B. Stuart, whose cavalry raids and reconnaisance in Fairfax County included the capture of Burke Station from which he telegraphed President Lincoln complaining of the quality of the mules he found there

Brigadier General Herman Haupt, who commanded the Union Army's military railroads and kept that transportation system operating to supply the Federal troops campaigning in Virginia. National Archives portraits; courtesy of Fairfax County Library Photographic Archive

Brigadier General Irvin McDowell, commander of the Union army at the First Battle of Bull Run whose defeat there led to construction of a massive network of fortifications in Northern Virginia to protect the nation's capital

Major General John Pope, commander of the Union forces at the Second Battle of Bull Run, whose defeat opened the way for the Confederate army under Lee to invade Maryland in the summer of 1862

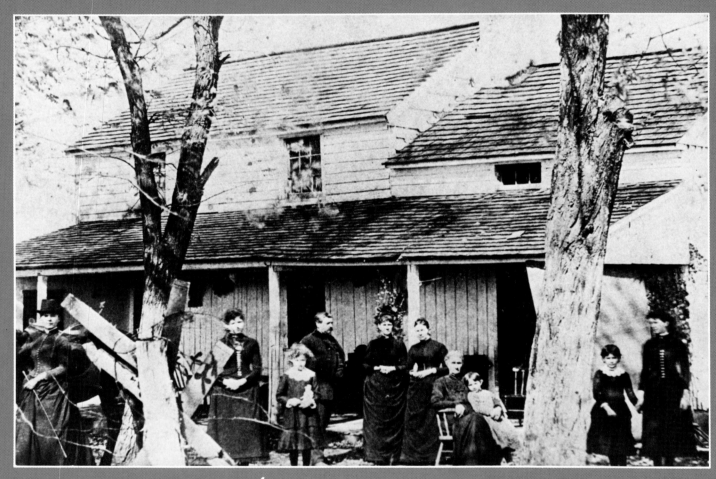

Although many of its residents left Fairfax County after the Civil War and sought better opportunities in the West, many others stayed on the land their families had occupied before and worked to rebuild their fortunes. Typical of this latter group was the Farr family of Dranesville. Shown here about 1900, with three generations represented, members of the family pose in front of the homestead that had been built early in the 1800s and had, at various times, housed a tavern, a school, a post office, a store, and a surveyor's office. Courtesy of Fairfax County Library Photographic Archive

CHAPTER 6

The Years of Rebuilding: 1865-1890

Although Fairfax County suffered greatly from the constant patrolling, raiding, skirmishing, and destruction of civilian property that took place there during the war, it was in some respects better equipped than other parts of the South to recover when peace was restored. It was located adjacent to a growing urban market for agricultural products; it was in both the overland and river transportation corridors of the East Coast; and it was the beneficiary of a substantial migration of newcomers, chiefly from New York, New Jersey, and Massachusetts. These people were attracted by cheaper land, less congestion, and a more agreeable climate. The newcomers added to the number, the vigor, and the capital resources of Fairfax County's residents in the years of rebuilding that lasted roughly from 1865 to 1890.

In this period, new directions were taken in local government as the Virginia Constitution of 1869 replaced the old county court administrative system with the board of supervisors. Past tradition was also broken by providing for a system of free public schools. County political debate reflected disagreements at the state level regarding who should be responsible for Virginia's prewar bonded debt (some $45 million in 1875) and for the large number of paupers, indigents, and handicapped people left by the war.

In politics, Fairfax County's newspapers of this period—the *Fairfax News,* and later the *Fairfax Herald*—took conservative positions, even to the point of seeming to cling too long to The Lost Cause and fan the fear that chaos would reign if Republicans ever were permitted to come to power. But in this respect the editors seem to have lagged behind public willingness to adopt new attitudes and ways to put the county's social and economic systems in working order. After the initial years of Reconstruction, Fairfax County was represented in the Virginia General Assembly and the United States Congress by the same families that had supplied its leaders since colonial times. In the new offices of local government, however, the Northern newcomers began to appear in key positions and to inject new vigor and commitment into county, town, and village life.

As recovery progressed, Fairfax County resumed the appearance of a quiet, evenly paced agricultural region. Yet in these years the emergence of a number of new communities, mainly along the railroads, provided contrasts to life on the farm and a clue to the direction of future growth. On the farm, also, the seeds of change could be seen growing in the activities of farmers' organizations dedicated to the enhancement of social and economic conditions and improvement of husbandry.

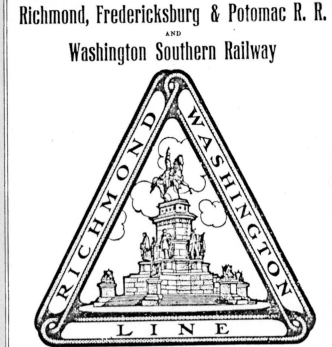

Richmond, Fredericksburg & Potomac R. R.
AND
Washington Southern Railway

LINE

W. P. Taylor, Traffic Manager

THE DOUBLE-TRACK LINK CONNECTING THE

Atlantic Coast Line Railroad
Baltimore & Ohio Railroad
Chesapeake & Ohio Railway

Pennsylvania Railroad
Seaboard Air Line Railway
Southern Railway

Between All Points via Richmond, Virginia, and Washington, D. C.

The Gateway Between the North and the South

Fast Mail, Passenger, Express, and Freight Route

During the early years of railroad construction, Richmond interests organized the Richmond, Fredericksburg and Potomac Railroad and began to lay tracks north to Fredericksburg. By the time of the Civil War their road had reached to Aquia Creek, where passengers and freight were transferred to steamers to make the remainder of the trip to Washington by river. This arrangement continued through the war years as the Union armies operated a small navy of river steamers shuttling between Aquia and Washington more efficiently than wagon convoys could cover that distance. Finally, in 1872, through-rail service on the line was opened from Richmond to Washington as a result of the Pennsylvania Railroad's purchase of the rights to build a connecting line from Alexandria to Fredericksburg. This led to an economic war as the RF&P retaliated by expanding its line to Quantico Creek and improving its steamship service. This contest continued until 1890 when mergers cleared the way for a new line, to Washington Southern. Courtesy of Southern Railway

Efforts to reestablish rail service between central Virginia and the Alexandria-Washington area after the Civil War resulted in consolidation of several railroads that earlier had influenced the growth of Fairfax County. The Orange and Alexandria Railroad and Manassas Gap Railroad merged to become the Orange, Alexandria and Manassas Railroad. Then from 1871 to 1876, under the name of Washington City, Virginia Midland & Great Southern Railroad Company, it became a southern extension of the Baltimore and Ohio Railroad. Bankruptcy intervened from 1876 to 1880. Then, in 1881, the system emerged as the Virginia Midland Railway Company. In 1894 the Virginia Midland merged with the Southern Railway system. Courtesy of Virginia State Library

Joseph Thornton's letter, shown here, in which he agreed to assist in reconstruction of the Alexandria, Loudoun and Hampshire Railroad, illustrates the determination of Northern Virginians to rebuild their economy. In the case of the AL&H, however, it appeared that west of Vienna practically everything had to be started over. Bridges were out, tracks were torn up, and grades had been changed by the ravages of war and nature. In 1870 the AL&H was reorganized as the Washington and Ohio Railroad and a new route to the Blue Ridge was laid out. Even this effort proved to involve unforeseen difficulties and more reorganizations and mergers occurred until in 1894 the line was absorbed into the sprawling Southern Railway system (Harwood, Rails). From Loose Papers, Board of Public Works; courtesy of Virginia State Library Archives

Throughout the years of rebuilding the Civil War's damage, poor roads plagued Fairfax County farmers, and, in the decade of Reconstruction there were serious shortages of wagons and horses that could be spared for daylong trips to Washington or Alexandria. In the area along the Potomac from Occoquan River to Great Hunting Creek, some of this farm-to-market transportation gap was taken up by river steamers, as shown above in the notice of farmers' accommodations. Equally prominent is the advertisement of excursions to Mount Vernon, attesting to the popularity of George Washington's estate among residents as well as visitors to Northern Virginia. Courtesy of Frederick Tilp

Fairfax County was almost entirely rural in character, and in the years of reconstruction many families had only their farm wagons for transportation. By the 1880s, however, advertisements of buggies and surreys and spring wagons reflected the general improvement of economic conditions. Courtesy of Fairfax Herald

The internal conflicts that divided Fairfax County during the 1860s and '70s remained just beneath the surface of Virginia politics in the 1880s. The greatest political advantage a candidate in Fairfax County could have was the right to add "C.S.A." (Confederate States of America) after signing his name, particularly if his name was preceded by "Col." or "Gen." Only if the name itself was "Lee" could one's advantage be enhanced. All these advantages were possessed by General William Henry Fitzhugh "Rooney" Lee, the son of Robert E. Lee who after the Civil War settled at Ravensworth near present day Annandale. He entered politics and served as a State Senator, after which he was elected to three terms in the U.S. House of Representatives. The photograph shown at left is that of a painting hanging in Fairfax County Courthouse. His cousin, Fitzhugh Lee at right, originally of Fairfax and later a cavalry commander in the Army of Northern Virginia, was elected governor of Virginia in 1885. Courtesy of Fairfax County Library Photographic Archive

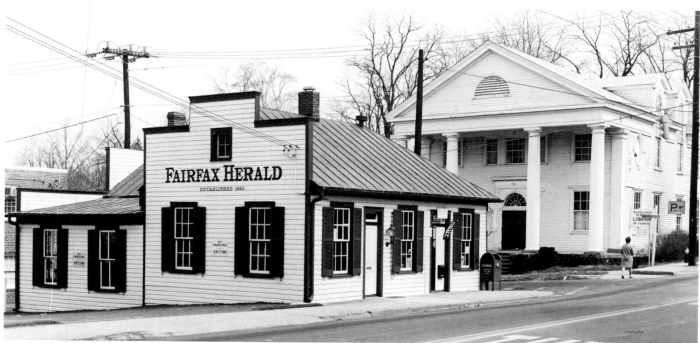

Captain R. S. Donohoe of Alexandria set up a hand-operated press in 1882 and began to publish the Fairfax Herald, *a weekly county newspaper which continued under its subsequent owner, William F. Carne, until it was bought out by publisher William Elvin of the* McLean Providence Journal *in 1973. It was an influential means of communication in the county for nine decades, carrying local and national news, neighborhood columns from communities all over the county, and government and legal notices from the Board of Supervisors, lawyers, and the County Court (Rust, Fairfax).*

Shown in back of the Herald *office is the old Town Hall which houses the Huddleson Memorial Library. It was built by Joseph E. Willard about 1900 and is now leased occasionally for social functions. William Edmund Barrett photo, 1971*

In the decades following the Civil War, lack of medical facilities greatly magnified the problems of coping with disease and preserving public health. William Benjamin Day of Dranesville was among the few country doctors who served families in the rural areas. During the Civil War, Dr. Day had been a strong advocate of secession and had served as a surgeon for the Sixteenth Virginia Regiment. He had been confined to the Old Capitol Prison in Washington on suspicion of being involved in the mysterious killing of two Union pickets. Eventually freed in an exchange of prisoners, Dr. Day left the area to serve as a surgeon in Cobb's Georgia Legion. After the war he returned to Mayfield, his home in Dranesville, and, during the 1870s and '80s, he became one of the most prominent and respected doctors in Fairfax County (Poland, Dunbarton). He was also a member of the first elected Board of Supervisors in 1870. The photographs here show Dr. Day and Mayfield in the 1880s. Courtesy of Eleanor Lee Templeman and Arlington County Library

Virginia had no tradition of public education, and the first decade of its public school system reflected the political turmoil and shortage of funds that prevailed statewide. In the 1880s, however, determination grew to make public education a success. In Fairfax County this era began in 1886 when Milton D. Hall was appointed Fairfax County Superintendent of Schools. He served in that office for forty-two years. Under his leadership the system grew, the first public high schools were established, and student transportation was begun (Legato School, *Wrenn, Peters, and Sprouse, eds.*). *Courtesy of Fairfax County School Board*

Miss Lillian Millan was a teacher at the Legato School for many years prior to the school's closing in 1929. During much of this time, her class consisted of thirty to forty students ranging from five or six years to twenty years of age (Legato School). *Courtesy of Fairfax County School Board*

In 1970 when Fairfax County celebrated the one hundredth anniversary of public education in Virginia, one of the centennial goals was to establish a school museum. The Legato School, built about 1877, and one of the few remaining one-room schools in the county, was moved from its original location on Route 29-211 between Fairfax and Centreville and restored. It is shown above at its present site in the county's government complex (Legato School). *William Edmund Barrett photo*

Faced with rebuilding the farms and orchards destroyed during the war, Fairfax County farmers sought strength through organization of clubs for education and cooperation in agricultural interests. Unlike the scientific farming societies of the 1840s and '50s, however, these clubs took up causes such as campaigning for better control of foxes, stray dogs, and other predators, and improvement of farm-to-market roads. The clubs were influential in persuading many farmers to switch from field crops to garden, orchard, and dairy and chicken produce that could be sold in Washington and Alexandria markets. Courtesy of National Archives

For a century—from 1870 to 1970—the unique and striking mansion known as Maplewood presided majestically over its location near Tysons Corner. The land on which it stood had been owned earlier by the families of Fairfax, Scott, Lee, and Gantt, and the first house of significance built on the land was called Strawberry Vale. During the Civil War it was the site of Fort Head, a Union stockade and signal tower, since it was the point of highest elevation in Fairfax County. In 1865 the property was bought by John Shipman who, about five years later, built a handsome brick mansion and named it Villa Nouva.

In 1884, Shipman sold Villa Nouva to General William McKee Dunn, a former Member of Congress and developer of the Dunn Loring community near Falls Church. General Dunn changed the name of the property to Maplewood and the house became the center of a prosperous farm. Following its sale in 1910 by General Dunn's widow, Maplewood served as the residence of a series of owners, some of whom made changes in the details of the house to enjoy it more fully, and some of whom gave it relatively little attention because of their

absence for long periods of travel.

In the 1950s, Maplewood was a successful dairy farm, but in the 1960s the farm was fragmented for highway construction, and in 1970 the owner, Colonel Rudolph Seeley, consented to have the mansion razed to make way for an office building for Westgate Industrial Park. With the demolition of Maplewood, Fairfax County lost its only example of the distinctive architecture of the French Second Empire and a landmark of the county's history (Rafuse, Maplewood). Jane Robinson photo; courtesy of Fairfax County Library Photographic Archive

*The activity at Camp Alger profoundly
affected daily life in Falls Church and its
nearby communities. In the summer of
1898 upwards of 23,000 men were encamped a mile and a half from Falls
Church. Units that did not arrive at the
railhead in Dunn Loring left their train
at Falls Church and marched through
the town. Troops on training marches
plodded through the outskirts of town and
along the country roads. Most visitors to
the camp from Washington came by the
trolley to East Falls Church and then
went to camp on foot or by horse and
buggy. The scene shown here was typical
of the traffic jams that resulted at the
East Falls Church trolley station (Steadman,* Falls Church)*. Courtesy of Falls
Church Historical Commission*

CHAPTER

7

The Capital Connection: 1890-1920

The introduction of steam railroads in the mid-nineteenth century was hailed as the most important advance in transportation in Northern Virginia since the rolling roads of colonial times. Yet these railroads were primarily concerned with connecting Alexandria and Washington with the Shenandoah Valley and Richmond. Although they fostered the growth of several new communities such as Clifton, Burke, and Herndon, and linked Fairfax County's farmers to more distant markets for their crops, the steam trains did not have much direct impact on the daily lives of county residents. During the nineteenth century, travel from most of Fairfax County into Alexandria and Washington was by horsepower, and a round trip took the better part of a day. All this was dramatically changed by the electric railway or trolley which appeared in Fairfax County as the nineteenth century turned into the twentieth.

The electric trolley was ideally suited to move people rapidly, regularly, and cheaply. Since a trip of fifteen to twenty miles could be accomplished in a matter of minutes, it became possible for Fairfax County residents to work, go to school, shop, and participate in activities in Washington, Alexandria, and Georgetown. Moreover, it was a two-way traffic. Residents and visitors to Washington came in growing numbers to enjoy outings at Mount Vernon, Great Falls, or, in 1898, to see a friend or relative among the Spanish-American War volunteers who were mustered at Camp Alger near Falls Church. These electric trolleys turned out to be a strong force in shaping the lifestyle of Northern Virginia in the first quarter of the twentieth century.

Along with the trolley, electric lights, telephones, and a host of other labor-saving devices were introduced. By 1920, even the remote rural parts of the county had some of these improvements. There was a new spirit of confidence everywhere. It could be seen in the establishment of schools such as the Jefferson Institute and Miss Mattie Gundry's Home and Training School for Feeble Minded, both in Falls Church, and in Ivakota, Dr. Kate Waller Barrett's mission farm near Clifton for rehabilitation of outcast girls. Pride prompted committees to install new street lighting, and places like Clifton that already had kerosene street lamps replaced them with electric lights. Many churches that had had only minimum maintenance for decades past were refurbished, modernized, and expanded.

This period of energetic and confident growth made its final surge in World War I. Public support of American participation in the war was strong in 1917 and was expressed by civilians in war-related work and fund raising, as well as by those who were in military service. An apparently unlimited demand for workers of all types throughout Northern Virginia led to individual opportunities never known before. This was especially true in the case of women.

Later, however, disillusionment replaced enthusiasm and President Wilson's idealism. Wartime sacrifices of civilian conveniences, the fresh graves in Arlington Cemetery, and strains resulting from efforts to grant at home the same civil rights that America purported to be fighting for overseas, the influenza epidemic of the winter of 1918-19, and a general unreadiness to digest so much social and economic change so rapidly, all contributed to the reaction that prevailed in the Roaring Twenties.

Supplies of all sorts to feed, house and equip the troops at Camp Alger poured into the freight depot at East Falls Church in the summer of 1898. To guard these supplies and reduce the disturbance of the peace by the steady stream of soldiers going to and from Washington through the town, a detachment of Camp Alger's Provost Guard was stationed at East Falls Church. Its tents are shown here pitched near the railroad siding. Courtesy of Falls Church Historical Commission

*F*ollowing the sinking of the battleship Maine *in Havana harbor in February 1898 and the declaration of war against Spain in April, a call for volunteers was issued. Overnight the Army's quota was filled and President William McKinley selected a site between Falls Church and Vienna for the first assembly point. The site was intended to be symbolic of a reunited North and South dedicated in common cause. Further, it was handy to Washington, connected by both steam railroads and electric trolley lines. In the* summer of 1898 thousands of volunteers trained in this facility, known as Camp Alger in honor of Secretary of War Russell A. Alger, who, coincidentally, had served in Fairfax County with the Union Army during the Civil War.

Military units whose names won fame in the Civil War were represented—from Virginia, the Richmond Blues and Richmond Grays, the Lynchburg Home Guard, and Danville Grays, and from the North, the Eighth Ohio, and the New York Volunteer Cavalry. One unit, known as the Fairfax Light Infantry, was raised by Captain Joseph E. Willard, owner of Willard's Hotel in Washington and son of Civil War Major Joseph C. Willard and Antonia Ford. It was mustered into the Army as Company I, Third Virginia Infantry Regiment and is shown here assembled at Fairfax Court House prior to departure for Camp Lee near Richmond in May 1898 (Steadman, Falls Church). *From* Industrial and Historical Sketch of Fairfax County, Virginia, *1907*

The tent city that grew up at Camp Alger threatened to create conditions that neither the Army nor the local communities could tolerate for long. One threat was to the water supply. In Falls Church most households had their own wells, and several shallow wells were dug at Camp Alger. But lacking any adequate nearby stream, the Army eventually had to haul water from Washington in barrels.

The second, more serious threat came from disease due to the unsanitary conditions of camp life. Modern sanitary discipline was unknown and, like soldiers through the ages, the men washed clothes, bathed, and drank from any pond or creek they found. In camp, food was prepared in the open air, exposed to flies and dust. Garbage was emptied into open pits. The disorderly scene caught in this photograph was typical. Added to this were the poor quality of the rations—including hardtack that had been packed for the Union Army in 1864—and inadequate housing —seven by eight foot tents, wall to wall, in which four men slept in blankets on the ground. Inevitably diarrhea and typhoid fever became major problems.

In the end, Camp Alger barely fulfilled

its purpose before it had to be closed and the troops transferred to posts with adequate medical facilities. But by this time, the bulk of the volunteer regiments that were destined for campaigning in Cuba had been mustered, organized, and

sent to their next post for training. As the summer of 1898 ended, Falls Church and its neighbors settled back into a more leisurely way of life (Steadman, Falls Church). Courtesy of Fairfax County Office of Comprehensive Planning

In the 1890s, the electric railway—the trolley car—was perfected, and trolley car lines reached out from Washington in all directions. In Northern Virginia the rail system connected the capital with Alexandria, Mount Vernon, Arlington, Clarendon, Falls Church, and Fairfax Court House. The equipment used on these lines sometimes was unusual; the Washington, Arlington, and Falls Church Railway is reported to have started with secondhand streetcars and horsecars.

This state of affairs attracted the attention of two energetic and resourceful promoters—John McLean (shown here) and Stephen Elkins. In particular they looked at the Great Falls of the Potomac and its undeveloped potential for one-day outings that were popular at that time. It had scenery, the old Patowmack Canal, the village of Matildaville, and, also very important, the land between Washington

and Great Falls was largely uninhabited and easily developed.

John McLean was a millionaire, active in Washington real estate, owner of the Washington Post and Cincinnati Enquirer, and patriarch of a famous Washington society family that included Evelyn Walsh McLean, onetime owner of the Hope Diamond. Senator Stephen Elkins had founded a coal, lumber, and railroad empire in West Virginia and was a U.S. senator from that state.

McLean and Elkins acquired the Great Falls site and started work on an electric railway linking it with Washington. In January 1900 they organized the Great Falls and Old Dominion Railroad. By the summer of 1906 the line started operations to Great Falls Park where McLean and Elkins had built a dance pavilion, a merry-go-round, and picnic sites overlooking the falls (Williams, W&OD). Courtesy of Ames Williams

The "Dyke," a favorite resort for fishermen and hunters on the line of the Mt. Vernon Railroad, near Alexandria, Va.

The Great Falls and Old Dominion Railroad was an immediate success. Crowds flocked to the park in such numbers that additional rolling stock was needed. As a stopgap, three small steam locomotives and six open-end wooden coaches were obtained to supplement the strained electric trolleys on weekends. The steam equipment, shown here, had served on New York City's original elevated railroad system and had been retired when that system was electrified. As used on the GF&OD, the little steam engines pulled two cars, the second of which was equipped with a trolley pole to provide electric lighting in the coaches. Notwithstanding this necessity to improvise, the GF&OD by 1907 was carrying 1.6 million passengers a year.

Communities grew up and prospered at several locations along the line. The community of McLean, named for the company's co-founder, grew enough by 1911 to warrant its own post office. The mail was, of course, delivered by the trolley (Williams, W&OD). Courtesy of Ames Williams

The electric railway line from Alexandria to Mount Vernon inspired not only visions of new communities but ideas for recreation in the natural setting of the river. One particularly popular site easily accessible by the trolley was The Dyke near Hunting Creek. Presumably the Alexandria Gazette described a typical outing when it reported that "a fishing party of six...spent yesterday at the dyke on the opposite side of Hunting Creek. They carried with them six gallons of liquor and returned with none. One of them, it is said, ate a gallon and a half of Chowder." (Netherton, Montebello). Post card printed by T. F. Ellis, Mount Vernon, Virginia; courtesy of Edith Sprouse

In 1920, Fairfax County's health and medical services were little better than they had been in 1880. Country doctors, like Dr. Alfred Leigh of Colvin Run, shown here in a 1916 photograph, were the only contact most people had with medical care or public health. Fairfax County established a public health code and appointed a board of health in 1913, but it was not until the worldwide influenza epidemic of 1918-1919 that the public took seriously the need for health and sanitation. The need for doctors and nurses during World War I took most of the county's doctors, and Dr. Alfred Leigh was one of the few left to fight the epidemic at home. He himself died of influenza in the winter of 1918, one of 531 county residents who were victims of the flu. Courtesy of Hassell Leigh; copy by Bernie Boston

For over 300 years, Virginia's rural roads had had a worldwide reputation for dissolving into a sea of sticky clay in wet weather. This scene was photographed near Fairfax in 1911 and depicts a situation that led the public to organize serious efforts to improve Virginia's antiquated system for administering local roads. Farmers who needed to get their crops and produce to railroad stations were among the leaders in the work for better roads, but the growing number of automobile owners during and after World War I also was a strong force in bringing about improvement of some of the older toll roads in Fairfax County. In an optimistic step, the Arlington-Barcroft Bus Company in 1915 established a "new jitney line" from the Aqueduct Bridge to Langley. By the early 1920s, several bus lines connected Washington and Alexandria with parts of Fairfax County (Reed, Fairfax County). Courtesy of Virginia Department of Highways and Transportation

Even at its best, the service of the railroads in Fairfax County was limited by the poor condition of the roads used for travel to and from the railroad stations. Historically, roadbuilding in Virginia had been the responsibility of the counties, and they had neither money, manpower, nor engineering know-how to build all-season roads. When the popular outcry for better roads rose in the early 1900s and became irresistible in the transportation demands of World War I, it was first answered by efforts to revive toll road funding. Attempts were made to rehabilitate some of the turnpikes of a century earlier and to realign or reconstruct other links in the county's farm-to-market network by bond issues to be repaid from tolls. By 1920, however, most of these toll road schemes had failed and other methods were being sought to develop a statewide highway system. For a brief period the automobile and the haywagon shared the road before the horse was finally replaced by the wave of popular demand for machines and smooth paved highways. Courtesy of Virginia Department of Highways and Transportation

Thomas Gantt, shown here in a miniature surrey pulled by his dog, Hobson, enjoys country living at Walney near Centreville in the early 1900s. Courtesy of Fairfax County Library Photographic Archive

In the first quarter of the twentieth century, the steam railroads enjoyed a period of expansion and relative prosperity as their service was demanded during World War I and thereafter by the steady growth of the city of Washington. Yet despite the railroad's success in providing transportation for Fairfax County's garden produce and dairy products, it did not stimulate the overnight growth of new towns that had been hoped for by its promoters. Most of the stations along the Southern Railway's line through Fairfax County continued to resemble isolated rural stops for the pick-up and delivery of freight. Fairfax Station, pictured here in a 1919 photograph, was typical of these places. From Southern Railway Archives; copied by William Edmund Barrett

Among the new communities established in Fairfax County in the 1880s and '90s, none was more colorful than Wiehle, laid out in the area of present-day Reston. In 1887 a German-born retired physician from Philadelphia, Dr. Carl Adolphe Max Wiehle, acquired about 3,500 acres beside the AL&H Railroad and laid out a self-sustaining planned community. As Wiehle took shape in the 1890s, it became a resort retreat for Washingtonians who came to visit the

Aesculapian Hotel. A. Smith Bowman, Jr., remembered the hotel as a "rambling 35-room building with towers, gables and many porches. It sported a bowling alley and tennis courts, the lakes afforded swimming and boating and the surrounding woods offered cool bridle paths and good hunting. [It] was filled to capacity each summer at monthly rates of $30.00 including board. Its chef had once worked for J. P. Morgan and its cuisine and the excellent quality of its spring water [were]

known for miles around. There was a continual waiting list" (Bowman, "Sunset Hills Farm"). Despite this success, Wiehle did not prosper as a permanent town and languished early in the 1900s after Wiehle died. Sixty years later the idea of a new self-sufficient town in this area was revived and realized in the community of Reston. Courtesy of A. Smith Bowman Distillery

Wakefield Chapel, shown here, is located near Annandale on land that was once part of the historic Ravensworth tract. It was built in 1899 mainly through efforts of two Union Army veterans who settled there and sought to counteract the lack of community facilities in that remote area. Initially, the church was reserved for Methodist services twice monthly, but it was also available for use by other church groups and other groups "for the further-ance of Christian principles" (Evans, Wakefield Chapel). The church was named in honor of its first pastor E. W. Wakefield, one of the founders. Even-tually Wakefield Chapel was added to the Methodist Protestant Fairfax Circuit which already included the Beulah and Vale churches near Vienna and Salem Church in Forestville (present-day Great Falls). No longer in use as a church, the building has been recently restored for community use by the Fairfax County Park Authority. Steve Behrens photo, Public Affairs Office; courtesy of Fairfax County Library Photographic Archive

Despite the demise of the Patowmack Company's canal and navigation venture, Great Falls continued to attract the interest of aspiring industrialists. In the 1850s, Thomas ap Catesby Jones with several others organized the Great Falls Manufacturing Company, and there was talk of harnessing the power of the river so as to rival the great mill and foundry towns of New England. These hopes never were realized, however, because of the intervention of the Civil War and the slow economic recovery that Northern Virginia experienced.

During these years of rebuilding, Matil-daville all but disappeared, overgrown by the forest that steadily encroached on the canal and its related structures. By the 1900s, Dickey's Tavern was the sole remaining link with the site's earlier times. Shown here about 1900, the tavern and its surroundings had changed very little in the fifty years just passed. For many years at the end of the nineteenth century, Dickey's Tavern was visited by some of Washington's most prominent residents and statesmen who ended a day of fishing with dinner at the tavern. From the James Watt collection; courtesy of Fairfax County Library Photographic Archive

Accotink School, shown in a 1907 photograph, was a step up from the one-room schoolhouses that made up Fairfax County's school system in the 1880s and 1890s. Despite increasing financial and moral support from both governmental and private sources and a recognized improvement in the quality of education, the county had poor school attendance. In 1900 it ranked ninety-eight out of 100 counties in the percentage of its school-age population attending schools. To a great extent this was due to the large number of students who rode the electric trolleys into Washington to attend classes in that city's schools. From Fairfax County, Virginia, *1907*

The first decades of the twentieth century were the heyday of the one-room school, and in Fairfax County they were the scene of a great achievement in public education. The census of 1900 reported that almost 16 percent of the population was illiterate, and in 1910 almost 11 percent. But in 1920 only 4 percent could not read and write, and the county ranked first in Virginia in literacy. The interior design of the Accotink School, shown here, was well suited to provide a wide range of special activities in addition to the basic reading, writing, and arithmetic. Accotink was one of a dozen schools that had a piano or organ donated by public subscription. From Fairfax County, Virginia, *1907*

The farmer's season of work began as early in the spring as weather permitted so that plowing would be finished before the ground dried out and hardened. Throughout the 1920s plowing was done with a team of horses and a single plow. According to Wilson McNair, who had a large farm near Floris, most farmers could plow only an acre and a half in a day by this method. This photograph shows spring plowing on the McNair farm in the first decade of the twentieth century (Pryor, Frying Pan Farm*). From Louise McNair Ryder; courtesy of Fairfax County Library Photographic Archive*

Woman's work at the beginning of the twentieth century in Fairfax County had changed little in fifty years. The farm wife was in charge of the house, the kitchen garden and chicken yard, and the family's canning, cooking, clothing, and child care. All this was done with few mechanical aids, and until well after 1935 few Fairfax County farm women had the luxury of electricity (VPI, The Housing of Virginia's Rural Folk*). Women's work was essential to successful farming, and inspired the almanacs to declare that "a farmer needs a wife like he needs the rain" (Pryor,* Frying Pan Farm*). The women here are at work at Dickey's Tavern near Great Falls. From the James Watt collection; courtesy of Fairfax County Library Photographic Archive*

Great Falls, located only about eight miles up river from the cities of Washington and Alexandria, offered a unique experience to residents of these urbanized places, and for their visitors. Even before McLean and Elkins, the promoters of the Washington, Alexandria and Great Falls Railway, discovered how scenery and entertainment could attract crowds to their amusement park and passengers for their trolleys, the falls were a favorite retreat for many groups.

These photographs illustrate typical activities of the 1890s and early 1900s. The group of ministers gathered for the annual Camp Meeting and Biblical Institute of the Methodist Church held at Great Falls in August 1910. The second group, unidentified, was typical of those that gathered for more worldly purposes, generally connected with fishing, camaraderie, and a brief escape from the regulated world of work and family responsibilities (Curran, McLean).
Courtesy of Fairfax County Library Photographic Archive

The nine-and-a-half foot monument of Richmond granite commemorating the death of John Quincy Marr, Captain of the Warrenton Rifles, was erected in front of the old Fairfax County Courthouse in June 1904. He had died at a courthouse skirmish with Union troops in 1861 and was the first Confederate officer killed in action in the Civil War. A graduate of the Virginia Military Institute, he had been a lawyer with a practice in Warrenton.

On the day of the dedication, the courthouse was crowded and speakers from Fairfax and Richmond gave addresses from morning until night, with time out for dinner. An account of the event stated that it rained all day "as in the days of Noah" (Fairfax Herald).

There is also an obelisk of Richmond granite memorializing all of the Confederate dead in the nearby Fairfax Cemetery. It is located northwest of the courthouse on Little River Turnpike. Courtesy of Lee Hubbard

High on the Potomac palisades above Great Falls, the Fairfax County Chapter of the Daughters of the American Revolution in 1912 placed a plaque recognizing George Washington's lifelong interest in navigation of the river. The plaque, shown here with the DAR members present at its dedication ceremony, reads: "In memory of George Washington of Fairfax County, Virginia, Patriot, Pioneer and Man of Affairs, who spent in developing his country the life he risked in her defense. This is exemplified in the Patowmack Company, incorporated to build the Patowmack Canal, of which George Washington was first president. Placed by Fairfax County DAR." Courtesy of Fairfax County Library Photographic Archive

*O*ne of the best known landmarks of the McLean area is The Blue House at the intersection of Old Dominion Drive and Old Chain Bridge Road. It was built in the 1890s by Matthew Laughlin, and was the center of his 700-acre dairy farm. Following breakup of the dairy farm, the building was used as a general store, an insurance agency, a law office; and, finally, in 1933, Clifton Laughlin made it the office of McLean's first real estate company. Today the third generation of Laughlin Realtors occupies the building (Curran, McLean). From Donie Rieger collection; courtesy of Fairfax County Library Photographic Archive

*O*rchards were numerous in the areas of Falls Church, McLean, Langley, and Dranesville in the early 1900s. Spring, summer, and fall each had its particular activities for the farm family, but none was more memorable than the cooking and canning of fruit as the summer ended. Then the farmhouse became the center of activity, and sometimes, as in making apple butter, it was carried on in great copper kettles set up over open fires outside. The farmhouse of the Eagraholm Orchard in McLean, shown here, is typical of the farm homes that were scattered through western Fairfax County in this period. In this picture Misses Eaton and Groves are standing on the back porch. Courtesy of Fairfax County Library Photographic Archive

*B*ecause Virginia's boundary with Maryland and the District of Columbia is at the high water mark on its Potomac River shore, the waters of the river always have harbored activities that were within reach of Virginians but not within the grasp of Virginia's officials. It was this way with the practice of anchoring houseboats in the river, a gangplank's distance from the shore, and offering there entertainment and attractions not so readily obtainable on dry land. Pictured here is Madame Rose's **Dream**, a transient business that flourished intermittently near Jones Point in the 1920s and 1930s. Allegedly it was the only two-story multi-girl house on the river (Tilp, Potomac). Courtesy of Frederick Tilp

In World War I and the 1920s, Fort Humphreys' motorized fire department, shown at left with its crew proudly standing by, was one of the finest in Northern Virginia. In addition to protecting Fort Humphreys, it also served the nearby rural communities in Fairfax County for which there were no volunteer fire departments. *Courtesy of Fairfax County Library Photographic Archive*

As World War I approached, the army moved its school for the Corps of Engineers from the Washington Barracks (now Fort McNair) to a small site on the peninsula in the Potomac known as Belvoir Neck. The site had been used as a summer training camp by the school since 1915, but, as expanded, it was named Camp A. A. Humphreys, after a Civil War Engineer officer. In 1917 it was renamed Fort Humphreys and its size was enlarged to cover the entire peninsula (10,000 acres). In 1935 it was renamed Fort Belvoir. *Courtesy of Fairfax County Library Photographic Archive*

During World War I, Camp Humphreys gave basic training and technical schooling to troops of the Army Corps of Engineers. Scenes such as the training shown in this picture postcard were typical of army camps throughout the country. *Courtesy of Fairfax County Library Photographic Archive*

101

*A*t a time when athletic programs were
rare in school curriculums, Floris Vocational High School proudly acclaimed its
basketball teams which won county championships in both boys' and girls' divisions
for several consecutive years in the 1920s.
Shown here, posing on the school's front
steps with their trophy, is the championship girls' basketball team for 1924-25.
Despite its small size, Floris Vocational
High School had a reputation for its
enthusiasm and competitive spirit as well
as its high academic standing (Pryor,
Frying Pan Farm). Courtesy of Fairfax
County Library Photographic Archive

8

New Times and New Ways: 1920-1950

The pace of the changes that had been started at the end of the nineteenth century speeded up spectacularly in the years 1920 to 1950. When Fairfax County emerged from World War I, it was predominantly a conservative agricultural economy wishing only to continue and prosper in that way of life. Thirty years later, emerging from World War II, the county's chief interest in land was for residential development and the chief concern of county government was to cope with demands for services and facilities that accompanied unprecedented growth.

As the 1920s began, the traditional family farm society faced a crisis. Farm labor was disappearing because of higher paying jobs in town. Rural transportation was becoming more expensive as railroads and trolleys grew less reliable and rural roads continued to be, in the words of one state highway commissioner, "six feet wide and nine feet deep" in bad weather. Farm life also lacked modern conveni-

ences. In 1920, only seventy-five out of 2,000 farms in Fairfax County had running water, and only 145 had electricity. Closer contact with Washington and Northern Virginia's towns often brought the temptation to "yearn for more than one could earn."

Reactions to this crisis varied. Some farm families sold out and moved away; others stayed but went to work in the city. Some tried to hang on to what they thought were traditional values by reviving the Ku Klux Klan and in other ways promoting white supremacy, narrow morality, anti-Semitism, and violent nationalism. The county's relatively small black minority suffered segregation as well as harassment on buses, curfews, and oppresive law enforcement.

In contrast there were constructive reactions to the changing times. With tireless and foresighted effort, Fairfax County Agricultural Agent Harry Derr turned farmers' interests to improving dairy herds and poultry. An improved strain of corn—named Fairfax County White Corn—was developed to produce up to ninety bushels an acre. Tractors and other new types of farm machinery increased, although up through the 1930s, horse-drawn implements predominated.

Farm family life improved. In 1926 the County Board of Supervisors provided funds for a home demonstration agent. Within a short time almost every community had demonstration clubs, 4-H Clubs, school leagues, chapters of The Grange, and similar groups offering instruction and carrying on projects for better family life, health, gardening and food preparation, and home and school improvements and beautification. Projects were started in both black and white schools. Radio station WJSV in Mount Vernon Hills gave air time for progams on farm topics. In 1931 the annual Piedmont Dairy Festival was started. By 1935 dairy and poultry farming produced gross profits of over one million dollars for Fairfax County farmers.

World War II increased the urban impact to a point where the end of Fairfax County's agricultural era was clearly in sight. By 1945 the population had doubled in the previous four years, and land was increasingly being appraised on residential value rather than on farm use. The needs of newcomers and the old farm-based groups were everywhere in competition and often were in conflict. Organizations were thought to be the key to success, and it seemed that every cause and interest brought new ones into being to plan, promote, propagate, and protect it. Generally, the County Board of Supervisors was the target of their attention so that it might truly be said that at the century's mid-point, in 1950, local government in Fairfax County was livelier and more vigorous than at any time in its history.

❧

In the rural atmosphere of the Floris community in the 1920s, musical groups sprang up spontaneously. The largest and most serious of these groups was the Floris Community Orchestra organized in 1928 by Miss Gladys Thompson, an elementary school music teacher. Recruited from Miss Thompson's own violin students and other musically inclined young people, the community orchestra consisted of twelve violins, and banjos, mandolins, saxophones, piano, and drums. In addition to its annual concert, the orchestra was in demand for school plays and other musical events. This group photograph was taken in 1929. The car in the background, a one-seated roadster, had a rumble seat in which Miss Thompson carried members of the orchestra to performances. The building in the background is one of the county's four-room schoolhouses (Pryor, Frying Pan Farm). From Louise McNair Ryder Collection; courtesy of Fairfax County Library Photographic Archive

"*I have a pack of six Walker-type hounds and some acres of land, that should be enough for a start.*" So said A. Smith Bowman, Sr., to a group of friends and neighbors in 1928. His estate, Sunset Hills, included over 4,000 acres of beautiful woods, meadows, and streams. The next year, the Fairfax Hunt was formally registered with the Masters of Foxhounds Association of America in Boston, Massachusetts, and the hunt country map was recorded. This early picture was taken of the members and their guests gathering for a hunt on a misty morning in front of the Bowmans' Sunset Hills mansion.

Eventually, because of intensive development in the western part of Fairfax County—Dulles Airport and Reston—the Fairfax Hunt was moved in 1970 to the Ashburn-Arcola area in Loudoun County (Opstad, Fairfax Hunt). *Courtesy of the Fairfax Hunt*

Because in some parts of Fairfax County the soil is quite thin, there was a constant need to restore its fertility by spreading manure in the fields between the growing seasons. Farmers who raised livestock were fortunate in having a steady supply of this fertilizer, and often one of the chores assigned to the boys in a farm family was to clean out the barns and haul the manure to the fields. This photograph, taken from the 1925 Annual Report of County Agricultural Agent H. B. Derr, shows two boys using a homemade wooden sled pulled by a team of horses to haul manure to the fields where they spread it with their pitchforks (Pryor, Frying Pan Farm). *Courtesy of Fairfax County Library Photographic Archive*

In the early 1900s, particularly during World War I, the demand for dairy products in the national capital area attracted many Fairfax County farmers to dairy farming. The organization of a milk producers' cooperative in 1916 helped improve the marketing of these products and the maintenance of quality standards. In the early 1920s the Maryland and Virginia Milk Producers Association was formed, and by 1923 it had 121 members in Fairfax County, representing herds of over 15,000 cows. The county agent's annual report for 1924 revealed that Fairfax County led all other Virginia counties in dairy products. The average milk production of the county's cows was more than twice the national average, and the Association's leading herd produced almost four times the national average.

Symbolic of this supremacy in dairy production was Sadie, the Holstein, pictured here after returning from a triumphant visit to the Virginia State Fair in 1924. Sadie was part of the herd of Ben Middleton, a Herndon dairyman, and she was said to be "the best known Holstein in the world" because of her production record—thirty tons of milk and one ton of butterfat in three years. At the height of her award-winning career, in September 1925, she was struck by a bolt of lightning and killed. From John Middleton; courtesy of Fairfax County Library Photographic Archive

The Agricultural Extension Service emphasized that practical application of training was as important as textbook learning. This photograph shows a cattle judging session on the Floris school grounds in 1950. Joseph E. Beard, who became Fairfax County Agricultural Extension Agent in 1937 on the retirement of Harry Derr, is shown (right foreground) directing the judging. The large shed in the background was built in 1918 and was regularly used for fairs and exhibitions sponsored by Floris Vocational High School, 4-H clubs, and the community (Pryor, Frying Pan Farm). Courtesy of Fairfax County Library Photographic Archive

Pat Middleton of Horse Pen Farm, near Herndon, was one of many farm youngsters in the 1930s to 1950s who maintained Fairfax County's reputation for prizewinning dairy herds. He is shown at a 4-H Club fair held at Frying Pan Park. Courtesy of Fairfax County Library Photographic Archive

Shortages of farm labor were for many years a restricting factor in Fairfax County's agricultural growth, and they were felt particularly during and after World War I. Everyone in the farm family was called on to do a share of the work. Yet in the 1920s before the establishment of an Agricultural Vocational High School at Floris, there was a general lack of means to teach farm women and children the improved labor-saving methods of their work.

Through the persistent efforts of the county's Home Demonstration Agent, Lucy Steptoe, clubs were formed to "learn by doing," and they provided opportunities for projects in cooking, bread-making, canning, sewing, poultry raising, gardening, home improvements, first aid instruction, and other subjects. While coordinated by the county's Home Demonstration Agent, these projects were supported by many other organizations, including the school leagues, railroads, 4-H Clubs, Chamber of Commerce, Daughters of the American Revolution, and others. This picture of Rebecca Rice of Oakton working on her home canning project is typical of the scenes throughout the rural part of Fairfax County in the 1920s and 1930s. Courtesy of Fairfax County Library Photographic Archive

Throughout history the women of farm families suffered most from the isolation of rural life, and this was one of the things counteracted by the Home Demonstration clubs, begun in the 1920s and '30s. Providing forums for the exchange of information about ways to improve farm home-life, these clubs offered unique opportunities for women of farm families to discover and use their talents in personal and group projects that enriched their lives and their families' lifestyles. The Floris Home Demonstration Club was honored in 1930 as the "most effective" club in Fairfax County; in this photograph its members are shown with their championship flag. Courtesy of Fairfax County Library Photographic Archive

Each year on Achievement Day Fairfax County's 4-H Clubs exhibited projects completed by club members. Throughout the 1920s and 1930s, as the farm-based communities of the county worked to adjust to the rapidly changing times, these activities focused attention and increased interest in such subjects as nutrition, home improvements, sewing, gardening, and public health. This photograph, from a report by Fairfax County Agricultural Agent H. B. Derr in 1930, shows the Achievement Day exhibits of the Oakton and Potter's Hill clubs. The Oakton project (left) displays "Unusual Ways of Preparing Our Old Friend Cabbage." The Potter's Hill display (right) exhibits hand towels and napkins designed and made by the club members (Pryor, Frying Pan Farm). Courtesy of Fairfax County Library Photographic Archive

In the years before the Civil War, the agricultural clubs provided forums in which Fairfax County farmers exchanged information about improved farming methods. In the years of postwar rebuilding and afterward, this function was performed by the Patrons of Husbandry, better known as The Grange.

The Grange that flourished in Fairfax County from the 1880s to the 1940s was more than a scientific farming club. It also provided a social outlet for farmers and their families, and at a national level it eventually became an economic and political action organization. Fairfax County's Grange chapters appear to have fitted into this pattern, for in 1886 the County Board of Supervisors gave permission to the "grangers and others interested" to erect a flagpole on the

courthouse lot for weather signals and flags, with a proviso that no political flags would be allowed.

Although in some states the Grange was associated with the Populist Party of the 1890s and 1900s, there is no sign that the farmers of Fairfax County were drawn to Populism by their Grange. The local Grange continued actively long after Populism ceased to be a political force, and it provided a particularly effective framework for farmers to obtain cooperatively some of the community services that the county government could not at that time provide. The scene pictured here shows a meeting of the Fairfax County Chapter of the Grange in 1940. Arthur Rothstein photo; courtesy of Library of Congress

Fairfax County's position of leadership in Virginia's agriculture was reflected not only in the state's annual production statistics, but also in the selection of officers of farm organizations and public bodies. Mark Turner, shown here in a photograph of 1940, was a Great Falls dairy farmer who was elected Master of the Virginia State Grange for three terms; for many years he served as a member of the Virginia Milk Commission. Arthur Rothstein photo; courtesy of Library of Congress

Edith Rogers, a teacher and dairy farmer of Herndon, who had been active in the Grange, was the first woman to serve on the Fairfax County Board of Supervisors. Originally appointed in 1935 to fill an unexpired term, she later was elected to the Board from the county's Dranesville District. Miss Rogers served at a time when both urban and rural interests were demanding attention, and she actively worked to harmonize these competing demands through progressive rural programs sponsored by the county's agricultural agent. Arthur Rothstein photo for Farm Security Administration; courtesy of Library of Congress

Publicizing Fairfax County's leadership in dairy herds and milk production, girls get ready to ride the county's float in the Piedmont Dairy Farming Festival parade in 1930. H. B. Derr photo; courtesy of Fairfax County Library Photographic Archive

The awesome power of the Potomac at floodtide has been seen regularly over the years at Great Falls. The scene shown here is from a picture postcard depicting the 1936 flood, which covered the main floor of the old Great Falls Inn and is the highest water mark attained since records have been kept—ninety-one feet above normal. Based on experience at Great Falls, it is expected that every ten years water will reach the top of the palisades, and every fifty years flood water will reach the second floor of the visitor's center. Courtesy of Fairfax County Library Photographic Archive

The Washington, Alexandria and Mount Vernon Railroad was built in 1892, and at that time, claiming speeds up to thirty miles per hour, was one of the most advanced electric trolleys in the nation. Until the 1920s it carried a steady stream of visitors to George Washington's Mount Vernon estate. The photograph here is of the WA&MV terminals at Mount Vernon about 1930 (Snowden, Some Old Historic Landmarks).

Expectation that the trolley would stimulate land development along its tracks led to starting the community of New Alexandria on a 1600-acre tract south of Hunting Creek. A furniture factory, a hotel, and about a dozen houses were built there, but a depression and a fire that destroyed the factory were setbacks from which the project never recovered. In 1924, in a sale in which William Jennings Bryan was the auctioneer, the remaining land of the developers was acquired by a group of buyers who later developed the Belle Haven Country Club and community (Risley and Dahlin, "New Alexandria"). From Joan Gibbs Lyon; courtesy of Fairfax County Library Photographic Archive

Historically, public libraries were as foreign to the traditions of Virginia as were public schools. Yet by the 1940s both were in demand. Prior to 1940 several towns in the county established community libraries with private support, and in this year the County Board of Supervisors moved to consolidate these facilities with a county-wide system. Town libraries served heavily populated areas and bookmobiles traveled to the others. The first bookmobile was a blue panel truck on loan to the county which carried about 600 books on regularly scheduled trips throughout rural neighborhoods. Courtesy of Fairfax County Library System

There were local units of the Ku Klux Klan in Fairfax County in 1868, but the high tide of the Klan in Northern Virginia came in the aftermath of World War I when the groups whose political and economic influence was based on their farmland were challenged by town commercial interests and newcomers who worked in Washington. Although membership in the Klan was secret, local units used public events to show off their numbers. This photograph shows a funeral in Fairfax Cemetery about 1929. Courtesy of Fairfax County Library Photographic Archive

A gold mine was operated on Bullneck Run in the vicinity of Great Falls from 1935 to late 1938 by Virginia Mines, Inc. Gold-bearing ore was blasted from tunnel walls some fifty feet below the surface of the ground and raised from the shaft in huge buckets. It was then loaded into ore cars to be carried 100 yards up the hill on a narrow gauge railway to the mill. In the mill, pictured here, the gold was extracted from the ore by breaking, crushing, and pulverizing the rock. The gold-bearing mixture was then passed over mercury-coated copper sheets where the gold would stick to the mercury, forming an amalgam. Finally, the amalgam was scraped from the copper plates and the gold was separated from the mercury. Photo, 1938, from the gold mining historical collection of Walter A. Goetz; used with permission

Shirley Memorial Highway, named to honor Henry G. Shirley, State Highway Commissioner from 1922 to 1941, was a wartime measure to relieve traffic congestion for the thousands of government workers who commuted between Washington and Arlington and Fairfax counties. When the first two and one-half mile section, between the Pentagon and Leesburg Pike (Route 7), was opened in 1944, it ushered in the expressway era of highway travel. The high-speed controlled-access highway, with landscaped roadsides and over-or-underpassed intersections, cost $1,268,000 when built. Eventually the state extended Shirley Highway south to Woodbridge in Prince William County. Courtesy of Virginia Department of Highways and Transportation

In 1982 the National Park Service celebrated the fiftieth anniversary of the Mount Vernon Memorial Parkway connecting Mount Vernon estate with Arlington Memorial Bridge. Constructed in 1932 to commemorate the bicentennial year of George Washington's birth, the parkway provides a spacious landscaped approach to George Washington's estate. At Arlington Memorial Bridge the road connects with the George Washington Memorial Parkway which runs along the Potomac palisades to the American Legion (commonly called "Cabin John") Bridge. Both parkways are under the jurisdiction of the National Park Service. Courtesy of Eleanor Lee Templeman and Arlington County Library

Civilian automobile travel was one of the first casualties on the home front in World War II. This photograph shows cars and trucks "frozen" because of the rationing of spare parts and fuel, stored in a farm field near Vienna for the duration. John Collier photo, 1942; courtesy of Library of Congress

During World War II, it was not possible to provide permanent housing for all the workers needed in the defense establishments located throughout Northern Virginia. Mobile home parks, like the Spring Bank Trailer Camp on U.S. Route 1 south of Alexandria, shown here grew up wherever space permitted. Spring Bank was named for a mansion (shown in the background of the photograph) that once had been owned by George Mason, grandson of the builder of Gunston Hall and author of the Virginia Declaration of Rights. Martha McMillan photo, 1941; courtesy of Library of Congress

In the list of Fairfax County's volunteer fire departments, the McLean VFD has the honor of being Company No. 1. While the town of Vienna had actually organized a local department earlier, McLean's company was the first to be officially incorporated. Prior to 1922 the McLean area, like other rural communities in Northern Virginia, had no local fire-fighting organization. Fires of all kinds were a constant threat. Volunteer action led to formation of the McLean Community Fire Association in the spring of 1922. Its first equipment was a two-wheeled hand cart fitted with a 200 gallon chemical tank and a borrowed extension ladder stored in a farm shed. In January 1923, a one-ton GMC truck and another chemical truck were bought. The company's first president, J. F. Beattie, donated an acre of land at the intersection of Chain Bridge Road and Cedar Street for a fire house built in the fall of 1923. At that time the only alarm system was a bell mounted on the fire house roof. This photograph shows the McLean Volunteer Fire Department's equipment on display in the 1940s (Curran, McLean). Courtesy of McLean Volunteer Fire Department

In the 1880s, telephone exchanges were established in Falls Church, Fairfax, Vienna, Herndon, and in the neighboring cities and counties. The numbers of subscribers grew slowly, however, until Dr. M. E. Church arranged for a line connecting his drug store in Falls Church with Washington and then provided a network of telephone exchanges in Falls Church, Fairfax, Herndon, Vienna, and Leesburg, and Loudoun, Fauquier, and Prince William counties. During the Spanish-American War, Dr. Church also provided telephone and telegraph service to Camp Alger near Merrifield. In 1916 this company sold its interests to the Chesapeake and Potomac Telephone Company which has provided service in Northern Virginia since that time. Shown is one of the manually operated switchboards serving Fairfax County in the 1940s. Dial service replaced manual switchboards in Fairfax County in 1954. Courtesy of Falls Church Historical Commission

Fairfax County is one of the few counties in Virginia that has its own police department. Carl R. McIntosh, shown here, served as police chief from the department's creation in 1940 until his retirement in 1957. Before 1940, he had been an officer in the county sheriff's department for many years. In its early days, the department depended on a motorcycle patrol to cover an area of over 400 square miles and the major highways that brought an increasing number of travelers to and through the county. In 1950, when the county's population was less than 50,000, its police force numbered fifty-six; in 1986, with the county's population standing at 649,000, the police department has a strength of 833. Courtesy of Scott Boatright, Fairfax County Police Department

Fairfax County's Motor Squad is part of its police department's Special Operations Division centrally based in the West Springfield Substation. The variety of specially trained and equipped officers in this division is a reflection of the county's wide range of conditions and situations that have to be handled by the police. In addition to the Motor Squad, the Special Operations Division includes a K-9 Corps of trained dogs, divers trained to work in scuba gear, park police, a Special

Operations Command (SOC) similar to the highly publicized SWAT teams, traffic and safety police, and a variety of investigative teams. Although the Motor Squad is most highly visible when called on for parades and escort duties, its members are highly trained in their primary daily duties of untangling traffic jams, patrolling heavy traffic highways, and investigating accidents. Courtesy of Fairfax County Library Photographic Archive

One consistent force helping to coordinate public support for economic development and community services was the Fairfax County Chamber of Commerce. In the 1930s, the Chamber and the Grange cooperated in promoting the success of the county agricultural extension projects. In the 1940s and '50s, the Chamber joined in working for improved health services, public libraries, transportation, and water systems. In its early years, the Chamber of Commerce provided a unique means of bringing together

representatives of the various parts of the county as well as the main professions and businesses. This photograph shows some of the members of the Fairfax County Chamber of Commerce about 1934 posed

in front of the old county clerk's office where, on the second floor, the Chamber and the Grange had installed an agricultural and industrial museum. Courtesy of Fairfax County Chamber of Commerce

The Floris Vocational High School was the third such school to be built in Virginia. It was constructed on a six-acre tract which George Kenfield had given to the Frying Pan School Association in 1876. One and two-room schools had occupied the site until 1920 when the two-year vocational high school was built. The citizens of Floris supported the vocational high school with money and by contributing their skills to the construction of the new three-story building and an agricultural shed nearby. For several years the Floris Home Demonstration Club served hot lunches at the school and sponsored the employment of a music teacher until county and state funds for this purpose could be obtained. In this photograph taken about 1950, the vocational high school (right) is shown beside the old Floris elementary school (left). Quentin Porter photo; courtesy of Fairfax County Library Photographic Archive

Wilbert T. Woodson served as Fairfax County's Superintendent of Schools from 1929 to 1961. He took over a mixture of one- and two-room wooden schoolhouses with potbellied stoves, outhouses, and waterbuckets, and modernized this school system to meet the spectacular growth in population and educational demands of his time. Woodson's foresight in encouraging and cooperating with community leagues, PTAs, and civic organizations led to the creation of a broad base of public support for high-quality education and administration and a wide range of special education programs. Courtesy of Fairfax County School Board

By the time of World War II, automobiles had decisively replaced railroads in local passenger transportation and motor trucks had become the farm-to-market connection in rural areas of Fairfax County. In this 1945 photograph, the Washington and Old Dominion Railroad's station at Dunn Loring is boarded up and beset by weeds. Courtesy of Fairfax County Library Photographic Archive

Fairfax County's first regional shopping mall was developed in 1953 on a thirty-four acre tract of land at Fort Buffalo, locally called Seven Corners. The land was owned by the heirs of Frederick Foote, a black with some white and Indian ancestors, who had purchased it for $500 in 1864. Before transfer to a developer could be arranged, a court order was needed to waive a provision of Foote's will that this land should never be sold outside his family. With this obstacle removed, the land was bought from the Foote heirs for $750,000. Kass-Berger, contractors in Washington, designed and built Seven Corners, and opened it for business in 1953. Few could have seen at that time how greatly these regional shopping malls would reduce the suburban resident's dependence on retail stores of Washington, but soon the major department stores and many national chains of stores established branches in the suburban regional malls. Moreover, in the case of Seven Corners, a major construction project modernized the highway facilities in its vicinity. When completed, Seven Corners was an immediate success and became the prototype for others that followed in the 1960s and '70s. Blue Ridge Aerial Surveys; 1982

CHAPTER

9

The Hub of Northern Virginia: Since 1950

As World War II ended, the national capital area did not shrink back to its prewar size and way of life—just the opposite. As Washington became a world capital, everything seemed to expand. Accordingly, Fairfax County became a place to live and a place to grow, both for the exploding population and for the business community that emerged to meet its needs.

The main things needed for these activities already were present. The county had undeveloped space and reasonable land prices. It had a location in the great urbanized East Coast crescent that was forecast to reach from Boston south to Norfolk with some of the main transportation corridors already laid out. It offered a stable, generally conservative tradition of government with moderate taxes. Family income and individual education levels were among the highest in the nation. And many citizens were concerned with the quality of the natural environment. Despite these assets, the 1950s, '60s, and '70s became

decades of hectic growth and growing pains.

Responses to these pressures came from every side. The county government was restructured by adoption of the county executive form. Recalling the lessons of prewar years, people organized to promote their interests, and now county-wide federations of organizations emerged to compete for attention—the League of Women Voters, Federation of Citizens Associations, the PTA, Northern Virginia Builders Association, and the Maryland and Virginia Milk Producers Association were among the early leaders.

Land development questions were at the root of most of this competition. For the time being, the art of local government consisted of finding ways of stretching the public facilities for schools, highways, sewers, and water to reach the subdivisions scattered over the county's open western parts. With the 1956 election, the Board of Supervisors became urban-oriented, and the land use problem was met by efforts at master planning and zoning.

Through the 1960s and '70s, new planning approaches were tried in both public and private sectors. Each had successes and failures. Regional shopping centers—the chief form of innovative private development—spread steadily after being introduced in 1953 at Seven Corners. The public sector's main innovation was the Beltway, taking the expressway design and bending it into a circumferential route that crosses the radial roads leading out from Washington and Alexandria. Travel anywhere in the county henceforth was reckoned in terms of minutes rather than miles.

The combined effects of these developments were striking. Major businesses shifted their head-quarters from Washington to locations in the county. The Central Intelligence Agency moved to Langley and the U.S. Geological Survey moved to Reston. Dulles International Airport, embodying Eero Saarinen's beautiful archi-tecture, was built on the county's western border.

Suburban housing and commer-cial development filled in the spaces that had separated the county's many small communities, and the county was threatened with a shortage of open space for recrea-tional use. Beginning in 1950, the Fairfax County Park Authority

public facilities for all forms of outdoor recreation and conser-vation of scenic beauty, augmenting similar efforts by the Northern Virginia Regional Park Authority and the park departments of towns and cities.

Concern for the brotherhood of man—something that often had been missing in earlier times—also steadily expanded in the county. Despite the periods of massive resistance to integration of black and white schools and to the Civil Rights Movement, minorities made progress in voting and ending discrimination in housing, public facilities, and employment.

Similarly the county's system for delivering health services to a population that in 1986 stood at about 649,000 received special commitments of both public and private resources. And in the area of cultural resources, the county enjoyed a unique combination of support from public and private sources. Beginning with county-wide groups promoting orchestras, choruses, and barbershop quartet singing in the 1950s, the groups participating in cultural activities now number in the hundreds. Facilities for these activities include George Mason University, North-ern Virginia Community College, and internationally famous Wolf Trap Farm Park, the only National Park devoted solely to the perform-ing arts.

Frank and Thelma Feighery bought their country store on Colvin Run Road near Route 7 in 1950. It represents a rapidly vanishing type of retail outlet which once could be found at almost every crossroads in Fairfax County.
Modern supermarkets like Giant,

Safeway, A&P, Magruder's, and others, with electronic price readers, have proven to be more profitable and efficient with their high-volume, low-profit-margin business, but they cannot compete with Thelma's delicious homemade ice cream or the handy self-service gas pumps.

Frank Feighery's 1953 antique Lincoln shown out front is frequently a trophy winner at auto shows. Richard Netherton photo

As more people moved into Fairfax County in the 1950s, their need for goods as well as services grew, and as residential housing patterns caused suburban sprawl, commercial facilities adopted styles that catered to shoppers driving automobiles. This view of a grocery store near Falls Church in the mid-1950s shows the usual response of merchants to the need for customer parking. Where space and money were available, barriers were installed between these roadside parking areas and the highway to improve traffic safety. All this, however, proved to be a very uneconomical use of land, and it led to the development of shopping centers and malls where a central parking area could serve a number of shops. Beginning in 1953, the small neighborhood shopping centers in Fairfax County were supplemented by regional shopping malls designed to serve market areas of up to 50,000 people. Porter photo; courtesy of Fairfax County Library Photographic Archive

On May 31, 1951, the Washington and Old Dominion Railroad ended its passenger service on the line from Rosslyn to Bluemont. Car 45 made the last run that day and is shown above receiving a rousing full-capacity farewell at the Falls Church station as it made its way toward Rosslyn. Termination of passenger service at a time when commuter travel to Washington was increasing dramatically now appears to have been a poor decision, but, with more than 100 grade crossings on its tracks, the Bluemont line faced a prospect of staggering expenses to provide for safety if it continued its operations (Harwood, Rails). Ara Mesrobian photo; courtesy of H. H. Harwood, Jr.

In the county election of 1955, a combination of redistricting and strong public reaction on the issue of regulating land development put the balance of political power in the hands of the urban-oriented elements of the county. Five of the seven seats on the Board of Supervisors changed hands and, in voting that crossed party lines, the new board began to handle the county's land zoning problems with a new respect for long-term consequences. As the new board took office in January 1956, Gib Crockett, political cartoonist of the Washington Star, presented his view of Fairfax County's board members in their characteristic poses. Courtesy of Fairfax County Library Photographic Archive

Illustrative of the wide support for construction of the Fairfax Hospital and the broad range of interests assembled to guide its development, is this photograph of the members of the Board of Trustees of the Fairfax Hospital Association in 1961. Seated left to right: Col. Raymond Rickard, banker; Donald Ball, building contractor and president of the Association; Honorable Jouett Shouse, former

Assistant Secretary of the Treasury; Wallace Carper, former chairman of the Board of Supervisors. Standing left to right: William Crossman, Jr., dairy farmer; Mrs. Euan Davis, member, Hospital and Health Center Commission; Dr. Lloyd Hazleton, founder of research laboratory; Mandley Rust, land developer; Mrs. John Lucas, civic leader and retired nurse; John Koons, automobile

dealer; Carl Soresi, editor; Walter Phillips, civil engineer. Not present: A. Smith Bowman, Jr., businessman; Norman Cobb, banker; Col. Davis Condon, Jr., Commissioner, Court of Military Appeals; Dr. Robert Hunt, pediatrician; and Carl Fritsche, research consultant. Charles Baptie photo; courtesy of Fairfax County Library Photographic Archive

Getting students to and from Fairfax County's schools in the 1950s and '60s required the use of a fleet of more than ninety school buses driving approximately 600,000 miles per year. It was said to be the largest school bus fleet east of the Mississippi River. In addition to their daily trip schedules, these buses helped enhance the county's school programs by taking excursions and trips to educational sites in the region. Jack Hiller photo, 1982

123

When plans for a Fairfax County hospital were begun in 1955, a fifty-bed facility was visualized. Six years later, after projected county growth and demand for health services had been more thoroughly studied, a five-story, 285-bed hospital was completed on the thirty-eight-acre wooded tract. On February 6, 1961, the Fairfax Hospital opened its doors one-half hour ahead of schedule in order to accommodate the imminent arrival of baby number one.

The growth of Fairfax County's population and that of the surrounding jurisdictions, has been augmented by births at the hospital. Between February, 1961 and December, 1981, 90,500 babies were born at Fairfax Hospital. A few of them were born in ambulances on the way there. In 1966 the hospital began issuing plastic umbilical cord clamps free of charge to the county's rescue squads after one newborn infant was brought in with its umbilical cord tied off with a piece of electrician's tape. Members of rescue squads, always equal to this particular emergency, had previously come up with other ingenious solutions to the problem which included string and cord, as well as rubber bands and even an occasional shoelace.

The ten-story addition shown here was opened in 1969, increasing the capacity to 656 beds. The Fairfax Hospital Association also manages Mount Vernon Hospital, built in 1976; ACCESS, an emergency and ambulatory services center in Reston, which opened in 1977; and Jefferson Memorial Hospital in Alexandria, acquired in 1985. A network of urgent care centers already includes facilities at Baileys Crossroads and Vienna. Fair Oaks Hospital is scheduled for a January 1987 opening. Courtesy of Fairfax Hospital Association

In the 1950s, Fairfax County's school population increased 238 percent. The number of school buildings rose from forty-two to ninety-three. The responsibility for planning, constructing, and managing these schools was the school board's, some members of which are shown in the 1959 photograph here. Standing left to right, Dr. Hillis Lory, Merritt Ruhlen, C. Turner Hudgins, and Dr. Merton Parsons. Seated are Samuel S. Soloman, left, and School Superin-tendent W. T. Woodson, right. The print in the back of the group is of the School Administration Office, now on Page Avenue. The county's spectacular expansion of its schools and the willingness of its voters to tax themselves to pay for a bonded debt of $69.5 million attracted nationwide attention as educators and administrators studied the results of this investment. Courtesy of Fairfax County Schools

Pioneers in the progress of education in Fairfax County were Taylor M. Williams (left) and Mona Blake (right). When the county established its first high school for black students, Luther Jackson High School in Merrifield, Taylor Williams was appointed as its first principal. He was a graduate of Tuskegee and American universities and had been an administrator in the school system prior to his appointment at Luther Jackson in 1954.

Mona Blake was the first black member of the Fairfax County School Board. She was a graduate of Howard University, and prior to moving to Reston she taught history in the Washington, D.C. schools. She served on the Fairfax County School Board from 1972 to 1974. Courtesy of Fairfax County Library Photographic Archive

Lake Barcroft was created in 1915 by placing a dam across Holmes Run at the old Barcroft Mill and Columbia Pike near Bailey's Crossroads to provide a reservoir for the Alexandria Water Company. In 1950, when the water company's needs exceeded this supply, it sold the reservoir and 680 acres of adjacent land to a group of New England developers who created a community of miniature country estates around the lake. Eventually, a community of over 1,000 families grew up there. Maintenance of Lake Barcroft's water quality, scenic beauty, and recreational potential have been a constant concern, and an active program to control soil erosion has utilized storm drainage and landscaping with soil-holding vegetation. A flock of Canada geese regularly makes its home at Lake Barcroft. Courtesy of Fairfax County Mapping Service

*As the rural character of Fairfax County
gradually was replaced by urban commercial and industrial development, farming
became an exceptional activity which was
successful only when it was carried out on
a large scale with labor-saving machinery.
This is illustrated in this photograph
which shows a line of tractors gang-
plowing a field at Sunset Hills farm near
the present location of Reston about 1959.
Courtesy of A. Smith Bowman Distillery*

*Although the Washington and Old
Dominion Railroad ceased its passenger
service in 1951, it continued to haul
freight on a steadily diminishing system of
tracks until its entire line had to be
abandoned in 1965. During these years it
traveled through parts of Fairfax County
where rural scenic beauty still reigned. In
this 1957 scene, a W&OD freight run is
passing the lake and Bowman distillery at
Sunset Hills near Herndon on its way to
Purcellville (Harwood, Rails). Courtesy
of H. H. Harwood, Jr.*

A. Smith Bowman, Sr., originally from Kentucky, wanted to return to farming after he made a fortune in Canadian wheat and the sale of his Indianapolis bus company in the 1920s. He bought the Sunset Hills farm in western Fairfax County in 1927, established the Fairfax Hunt, and raised cattle, horses, and grain. When prohibition was repealed in 1935, he established the A. Smith Bowman Distillery, presently the only legal bourbon distillery in the Commonwealth of Virginia (Wayland, Bowmans).

In 1961, Robert E. Simon bought almost all of the Sunset Hills farm of over 7,000 acres in order to begin his "new town" of Reston.

Bowman's sons carried on the family business after the death of their father. Here the late A. Smith Bowman, Jr., standing, and E. DeLong Bowman pose in front of a portrait of their father in hunting "pinks." Courtesy of A. Smith Bowman Distillery

In the 1950s, zoning matters demanded the greatest share of the Board of Supervisors' time, and the board created a planning commission to help guide growth and administer the zoning code. Keith Price, shown here, served as chairman of the commission in this turbulent period. As land developers scrambled to provide housing and commercial facilities for the newcomers moving into the county, they often were opposed by resident taxpayers seeking to channel growth into locations where sewer, water, schools, and roads could be provided most easily. The battleground on which they met was the planning commission where "Pappy" Price presided. Courtesy of Fairfax County Library Photographic Archive

In the 1940s, Edward R. Carr became convinced that the energetic growth of Fairfax County would soon turn in the direction of the Shirley Highway segment of the Washington-Richmond corridor. Already an experienced builder and community developer, active in the Washington area since 1925, he selected property along Shirley Highway which then was virtually virgin land. Here in the 1950s and '60s he developed Springfield, a business, commercial, and industrial community at the intersection of Shirley Highway and the Beltway. He also developed a series of smaller residential communities and recreational facilities surrounding Springfield. The success of these timely developments brought national recognition to Carr and Fairfax County for the quality of their planning and construction. Numerous honors followed, both for Edward Carr's leadership as a homebuilder and for his willingness to commit himself to civic activities and the arts. He died in 1974. In 1977, thirty years after he had founded the National Housing Center, he was elected to the Housing Hall of Fame located at the Center. The firm he founded, Edward R. Carr & Associates, was Northern Virginia's largest local builder in 1982. Courtesy of Edward R. Carr & Associates

*S*pringfield is one of the best known and most successful responses to Fairfax County's population growth in the years since World War II. Situated centrally in the county and divided in the middle by Accotink Creek, this area was until recently a pleasant Virginia countryside, well wooded and gently rolling, and Springfield was a whistle stop on the Southern Railway's track to Manassas and south. When Edward Carr began assembling land in that area, one local paper optimistically predicted that "Springfield will eventually contain over 5,000 homes, four schools, a huge shopping center and possibly an industry or two." Today these forecasts have been exceeded in a spectacular way. Later construction of the Washington Beltway, I-495, traversing the area east and west, made it a key location for interregional travel, and attracted all types of development in many times the magnitude its early developers predicted. These aerial photographs tell this story graphically as the scene in 1950 (left) is compared with that of 1981 (below). Blue Ridge Aerial Surveys photo, 1981; 1950 photo courtesy of Edwin Lynch

*A*lthough he gives credit to others for taking the first gamble of investing in central Fairfax County's open spaces, Edwin Lynch of Burke often is referred to as one of the developers of Springfield and a major influence on the present development of Burke and Annandale. The Lynch family came to Fairfax County around the turn of the century from Tennessee "with $6,000 to invest in Northern Virginia." They selected land in the Annandale area, became dairy and hog farmers, and continued to buy land. Today their farms provide the sites of Northern Virginia Community College, Springfield Tower, the Tower Shopping Center, the former Pinecrest Golf Course, and other area facilities. Ed Lynch, shown here, is now the patriarch of his real estate investment-management firm. He served as a member of the General Assembly and in 1952 was the last member to be elected to represent the entire Fairfax County in the House of Delegates. Courtesy of Edwin Lynch

*T*he Lower Potomac Pollution Control Plant was constructed in 1970 as an eighteen mgd (million gallons per day) secondary activated sludge plant. In the late 1970s it was expanded to a thirty-six mgd advanced wastewater treatment plant, the largest wastewater treatment facility owned and operated by Fairfax County. In contrast to earlier times, when soil erosion and siltation were the

main concerns, modern water pollution control must deal with complex problems of reducing phosphorus levels, suspended materials, and oxygen-consuming substances. The Lower Potomac Pollution Control Plant is located at the intersection of U.S. Route 1 and Armistead Road in Lorton. From Air Photographics, Inc.; courtesy of Fairfax County Department of Public Works

Subdivision and development of land depended on the presence of water and sewer facilities, and in the explosive growth of Fairfax County in the 1950s and '60s planning and paying for these systems often caused major controversy. When these issues were settled, however, there remained the formidable task of actually constructing these facilities. The large size of the pipe in this photograph is a reminder of the remarkable engineering and construction feats that were accomplished by the construction industry in meeting the service needs of county development. After the Fairfax County Water Authority purchased the Alexandria Water Company and its Occoquan Reservoir in 1967, ductile pipe like this along Keene Mill Road was laid to provide transmission mains to supply water customers.

Since the opening of the intake line on the Potomac River just inside of Loudoun County above Great Falls in 1982, the Water Authority has served about seventy percent of the county's water needs, fifty percent from Occoquan and fifty percent from the Potomac.

Sewer service is provided through Fairfax County's Department of Public Works. Courtesy of Fairfax County Library Photographic Archive

The sanitary landfill on 104 acres of land purchased or leased by Fairfax County since 1962 is located on West Ox Road south of U.S. Interstate Route 66. It was operated according to a design plan which has incorporated the most up-to-date sanitary engineering technology. When completed in 1982, this facility had accommodated more than 3,000,000 tons of solid waste, and has a top elevation of 575 feet, the highest land mass in the county. Also, it probably will make a prime site for archeologists of future generations who wish to study today's American culture. The elevation has been named "Mount Murtagh" after the designer of the facility. A new landfill at Lorton is now in use. Courtesy of Fairfax County Department of Public Works

Tysons Corner, at the intersection of two of Fairfax County's historic highways, the Alexandria-Leesburg Turnpike (Route 7) and Chain Bridge Road (Route 123), marks the point of highest land elevation in the county (515 feet). Maps collected by Richard Stephenson in his Cartography of Northern Virginia *show this name applied to the crossroads in the 1860s and that William Tyson owned land along the south side of the turnpike from a time prior to the Civil War. The picture taken in the 1950s looks south on Route 123 toward Vienna, and shows the Tysons Corner Store (one of the Good Will Food Stores chain built as an appendage to the building that earlier was William Tyson's house) and on the opposite corner the Crossroads Market. In the 1982 aerial photograph of the Tysons Corner area, Routes 7 and 123 cross each other in the right center of the picture with a grade-separated intersection and figure-eight interchange. Across the top of the picture is the Beltway (I-495) and vertically along the left side is the Dulles Airport Access Road.*

Today the complex at Tyson's Corner

is the largest concentration of business, commercial and professional facilities in Northern Virginia. Referred to since 1978 as "the downtown of Fairfax County," it includes shopping malls with individual shops and businesses, leading department stores, luxury hotels, resi-

dential and business condominiums, and high technology research firms. Early 1957 photo by S. R. Pearson in Donie Rieger Collection, courtesy of Fairfax County Library Photographic Archive; 1982 and 1985 aerial photos by Blue Ridge Aerial Surveys

This aerial photo, taken in September 1985, looking northwest, shows the West Park commercial and industrial complex, bounded by the Dulles Airport Access Road, upper right, and Dolley Madison Boulevard, in the foreground. Excavations for the new Tysons II complex are shown upper left, and above them, the Rotonda condominiums. Blue Ridge Aerial Surveys photo; courtesy of West Group, Inc.

Marcus Bles needed the giant stump axe pictured here to clear rights-of-way through Fairfax County forests in the 1940s, '50s, and '60s when his company performed contracts to dig water, sewer, and utility lines for new subdivisions. The equipment available was inadequate, so he invented this tool. Bles was successful in other ways. With intelligent foresight, he purchased large tracts of Tysons Corner in 1950 for an average of $1,500 per acre and later sold them at a comfortable profit to developers of the Tysons Corner Shopping Center and industrial park (Netherton, "Three Northern Virginians"). Courtesy of Fairfax County Library Photographic Archive

One of the major international organizations whose headquarters are in Fairfax County is the American Automobile Association. Founded in 1902 by nine auto clubs with fewer than 1,000 members, initially for the purpose of combatting the many unreasonable laws then in force to restrict use of automobiles, the association now consists of several hundred clubs serving more than twenty million members throughout the United States and Canada. Some of the AAA's early achievements include building public support for the first federal-aid highway law, posting route signs on U.S. highways, developing driver education in high schools, organizing the nationwide school safety patrol movement, and establishing the first national pedestrian safety program. Courtesy of American Automobile Association

Although the Central Intelligence Agency (CIA) was officially established by President Truman in 1946, it was not until fifteen years later that it got a permanent home on a tract of land in Langley, Virginia, used by the U.S. Bureau of Public Roads as a research station. President Eisenhower laid the cornerstone of the CIA headquarters building in November 1959 and the agency's first employees moved into the new building in September 1961. Today this building houses a wide range of activities gathering information from more than 150 countries worldwide about such things as oil production, grain harvests, weather, and population. In the corridors of the headquarters building are displays of paintings and other works of art on loan from the Corcoran Gallery of Art in Washington. Publications, maps, and atlases prepared by the CIA are available to the public, but tours of the headquarters building are not offered. In this photograph, the white domed structure in the foreground (lower right) is an auditorium. The brick buildings in the background (upper right) are the Federal Highway Administration's research station. Courtesy of Office of Public Affairs, Central Intelligence Agency

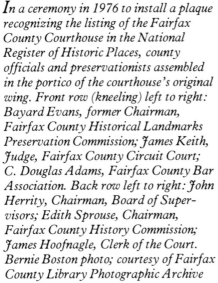

In a ceremony in 1976 to install a plaque recognizing the listing of the Fairfax County Courthouse in the National Register of Historic Places, county officials and preservationists assembled in the portico of the courthouse's original wing. Front row (kneeling) left to right: Bayard Evans, former Chairman, Fairfax County Historical Landmarks Preservation Commission; James Keith, Judge, Fairfax County Circuit Court; C. Douglas Adams, Fairfax County Bar Association. Back row left to right: John Herrity, Chairman, Board of Supervisors; Edith Sprouse, Chairman, Fairfax County History Commission; James Hoofnagle, Clerk of the Court. Bernie Boston photo; courtesy of Fairfax County Library Photographic Archive

James E. Hoofnagle was elected to an eight-year term as Fairfax County Court Clerk starting in 1976. Virginia-born and educated at the University of Virginia, he served in the Navy and as a United States Foreign Service Officer before coming to the administrative position with the county. During his tenure, under Chief Judge Barnard F. Jennings, all major functions in the circuit court have been modernized to save time, space, and reduce errors. Typewriters have been replaced by computers, and record keeping has gone from hard copy deed and will books to microfilm and microfiche, all meeting state archival standards. A new courthouse—the Judicial Center—was completed and dedicated in 1982. Warren Barry succeeded James Hoofnagle as court clerk in 1984. Photograph by Bernie Boston

*W*hen the urban county form of government was inaugurated in 1952, Carlton C. Massey was selected as its first County Executive. He served in that office until he retired in 1971. With experience as a civil engineer and local government manager, he supervised expansion of the county's services to deal with the problems of rapid growth and development in those times. As the county's population grew from 131,000 in 1952 to 469,000 in 1970, his budget reflected its increased demands, and rose from $10 million for all county expenses in 1952 to his last budget of $112 million in school expenditures alone. In contrast to the political controversies that marked state and county history during these years, Massey's administration was generally free from criticism and characterized by his good relations with the County Board of Supervisors. On his retirement the board named the county's new skyscraper government office building in his honor. Here, Carlton Massey is shown reviewing plans for this building which is under construction in the background. *J. Hamilton Lambert now serves as county executive. Courtesy of Fairfax County Library Photographic Archive*

*H*igh technology flies to the aid of Fairfax County residents aboard the Police Department's fleet of helicopters, inaugurated in 1983. Equipped with infrared scanners which penetrate foliage and darkness, a 3.5 million candlepower searchlight, night vision viewers, and advanced communications and radar systems, these helicopters greatly reduce the time and manpower needed for a wide range of police missions throughout the county's 399 square mile area. In a unique cooperative arrangement with the county's Fire and Rescue Department and the Fairfax Hospital Association, the Police Department gives top priority

*T*his 1982 aerial photograph shows the Fairfax County central business district and Fairfax County's new government center complex, a separate enclave within the city's boundaries.

The wing in the far right end of the old brick courthouse was the first unit, built in 1800 by John Bogue and Mungo Dykes, with additions constructed in 1934 and 1956 (Netherton and Waldeck, Courthouse).

The ell-shaped building, upper left, is the new Judicial Center completed in 1982; behind it stands the Adult Detention Center completed in 1978.

The tall structure in the center is the Massey Building, completed in 1969. It houses many of the county government offices needed to operate a county with over 649,000 people and growing. *Steven Moss photo, 1982.*

to rescue and medical evacuation missions, lifting patients and accident victims to medical centers in the national capital region. Although the crew for normal operations consists of a pilot and medic-observer, the Medevac helicopters can carry a flight crew of three to four, a patient, monitoring and advanced life support systems, and specialized medical equipment. Although the helicopters can land and take off from any clear area, some hospitals, such as the one shown here, have installed landing pads near their emergency entrances. *Scott Boatright photo; courtesy Fairfax County Police Department*

136

*M*ontebello, built on the old Lord Bryan Fairfax Mount Eagle estate south of Alexandria on Route 1, is representative of the development of condominium ownership of residential high-rise apartment building property. The system gained acceptance in the Washington area in the early 1970s when construction, fuel, and maintenance costs began to rise rapidly, making it unprofitable for most landlords to operate apartments as rental property.

The complex pictured above, which includes residences, a community center, health spa, and shops, also reflects changes in land use along old U.S. Route 1, where mom-and-pop restaurants and other small businesses are gradually being replaced by high-density commercial and residential buildings. Warren Mattox photo; courtesy of Montebello Associates

*S*tanding as a reminder of the growing importance of electronic communications in the computer-oriented work of modern industry and government, the American Telephone and Telegraph Company's regional communications center near Oakton also presents a striking example of excellence in modern architecture. In the center of this building is an enclosed atrium where full-size decorative trees and shrubs flourish in all seasons. The building was constructed in 1980. James H. Pickerell Associates photo

Although the Washington and Old Dominion Railroad ended regular passenger service in 1951, the very last passengers to ride its rails were Mel Marcey of Falls Church (left) and Alan Pennell of Leesburg (right). They built their gasoline-powered track car in 1969 with wheels that adjusted to either standard or narrow gauge tracks for exploring the abandoned railroads and spur lines throughout Northern Virginia (Williams, W&OD). Mel Marcey photo; courtesy of Ames Williams

The Huntington Metro Station, first of several projected stops in Fairfax County, was opened in December 1983. The Vienna Station was opened June 1986.

Construction of Washington's first subway/surface rapid transit system was begun in 1972. The first unit was opened in 1976. Completion of the first stage of 101 miles of track and eighty-six stations in Virginia, Maryland, and the District of Columbia is presently scheduled for 1993. Reggie Mason photo; courtesy of Washington Metropolitan Area Transit Authority

*F*air Oaks Shopping Mall, opened in 1980, is located at the major interchange of I-66 and Route 50, roughly in the center of Fairfax County. Fair Oaks includes regional and local retail, offices, research and development, a hotel, and multi-family residential facilities, including housing for the elderly.

Future planning for the surrounding area, much of it presently undeveloped, includes office buildings, light industry, a hospital, and a county government center. Steven Moss photo

*I*n 1874 Augustus and Sarah Brown deeded half an acre of land to the Methodist Church for a house of worship. Then Brown and his two sons proceeded to construct a church building. Known as Brown's Chapel, its first services were held in 1879, and it continued to serve an active congregation until 1967 in its location at Baron Cameron Avenue and Leesburg Pike. In 1968, the Northern Virginia Methodist Board of Missions offered the structure to the Fairfax Historical Landmarks Preservation Commission, which enlisted the aid of Gulf-Reston, Inc. in relocating it to a site on Baron Cameron Avenue opposite the entrance to Reston's Lake Anne Village Center. The church is not of the Victorian design that was typical of the time it was built but is of an earlier Greek Revival style found in New England where the Brown family originated. William Edmund Barrett photo

*I*n 1940 the noted architect Frank Lloyd Wright designed for Loren Pope of Falls Church a simple one-story residence of brick and cypress construction intended to furnish shelter while making the occupant aware of the freedom of space and a close relationship to nature. He called this style the Usonian or Natural House. Built in 1940 to 1941, the house was occupied by the Pope family and, after them, Mr. and Mrs. Robert Leighey until, in the mid-1960s, its destruction was threatened by construction of Route 66. To avoid this loss, Mrs. Marjorie Leighey donated the building to the National Trust for Historic Preservation which removed it to a site on the grounds of Woodlawn Plantation where it provides a forceful contrast in the architecture and life styles of modern America and the Tidewater plantation society. The photograph shows the Pope-Leighey House at its Woodlawn site. Courtesy of Eleanor Lee Templeman and Arlington Public Library

Woodlawn Plantation represents Fairfax County's commitment to preservation of sites and structures having historic and architectural significance. The Georgian mansion was designed by William Thornton, first architect of the U.S. Capitol, and built about 1805 on land that was a wedding gift from George Washington to his nephew Lawrence Lewis on the occasion of his marriage to Nelly Custis. The house is constructed in five sections and is surrounded by sweeping lawns and formal gardens. In the 1950s, the house was purchased by a group of preservationists who later gave it to the National Trust for Historic Preservation. Thereafter, it became the first of the trust properties to be opened to the public. As now restored, Woodlawn is listed in the National Register of Historic Places and included in a Fairfax County Historic District. Shown in the photograph above is an entry in the 1975 horses and carriage meet, one of the adaptive uses of the grounds that once were part of Woodlawn's farm fields. Charles Baptie photo; courtesy of Fairfax County Library Photographic Archive

Dorothy Farnham Feuer was the founder, in 1956, and the moving force behind the Fairfax Symphony Orchestra until her untimely death of cancer in 1963 at the age of thirty-four. A violinist, she worked tirelessly to help bring about the addition of a string program to augment the existing band instrument program in the county's public schools.

In recognition of her efforts, the orchestra's board of directors established the Dorothy Farnham Feuer Memorial Scholarship Fund which provides monetary awards to talented young winners of the fund's annual instrumental competitions. Courtesy of Fairfax County Library Photographic Archive

Beside Route 123 near Lorton prison youth center, the roadside plaque shown above marks the site of the Occoquan Workhouse where, in 1917, 100 women suffragists were imprisoned for demonstrating to demand the right to vote. Their willingness to go to jail and to go on a hunger strike aroused both the public and the politicians of the day to take women's rights seriously and helped lead to passage of the Nineteenth Amendment in 1920. The campaign to win recognition of the Occoquan Workhouse incident was spearheaded by Joseph Flakne, a civic leader working with Polly Noble of the Fairfax Area League of Women Voters, and Dr. Evelyn Pugh, a history professor at George Mason University. In March 1982 the roadside marker was officially installed and the site was added to Fairfax County's Inventory of Historic Sites. In the photograph Polly Noble (left) is shown with Congressman Norman Mineta of California who was the principal speaker at the dedication ceremony. E. A. Noble photo

It took twelve years for Swedish sculptor Carl Milles to design the thirty-eight bronze figures in the Fountain of Faith at National Memorial Park, located outside of Falls Church on Lee Highway at South West Street. Finished in 1952, it was the last of Milles' great works for which he personally supervised the installation. At the dedication of this memorial to reunion in heaven with departed friends and family, Milles said, "I hope it will be my masterpiece forever." According to William O'Neal, architectural historian of the University of Virginia, "Milles once more triumphed in this grouping of many figures and many jets of water achieving a subtle interplay of forms and a mystery through his juxtaposition of the motionless bronze and the flowing water. The Fountain of Faith is, without doubt, one of the nation's greatest fountains" (O'Neal, Architecture; Wrenn, Falls Church). *Also on the grounds of National Memorial Park is the Four Chaplains Memorial Fountain by Constantino Nivola, commemorating the heroism of four chaplains who died in the sinking of the* Dorchester *in the North Atlantic during World War II. Nan Netherton photo; courtesy of Arlington County Library*

Fairfax County Archeological Survey volunteers carefully scrape away layers of earth to locate artifacts and stains indicating undisturbed evidence of the county's past.

The county's Archeological Survey, headed by Mike Johnson, a specialist in prehistoric periods, and Sue Henry, specializing in historic times, and assisted by over 4,000 hours of supervised volunteer time annually, has been a leading force in preserving and interpreting physical evidence of over 11,000 years of human life in this area. This program, presently part of the Heritage Resources Branch of the county's Office of Comprehensive Planning, was established in 1978. Since that time it has located and preserved numerous sites, features and artifacts not hitherto recorded, and has made Fairfax County one of the nation's leaders in surveying and mapping its archeological sites, with over 900 on record.

Essential to the success of these programs is the enthusiastic citizen participation which has been encouraged by offering training courses to teach volunteers good archeological methods for both field and laboratory. Courtesy Fairfax County Archeological Survey

The nation's first national park for the performing arts is Wolf Trap Farm Park located near Vienna on ninety-five acres of land, the gift of Mrs. Jouett Shouse to the National Park Service in 1966. Four years earlier, Mrs. Shouse gave land and buildings at her Wolf Trap Farm to enable the American Symphony Orchestra League to establish its national headquarters in the national capital area. With her gift of land and money to the Park Service, an outdoor theater with an opera-size stage and seating for 3,500 was built. Additional space for 4,000 more people is provided on the gently sloping lawn outside the theater. The Filene Center and a smaller children's theater in the woods offer performances by local and internationally known artists and a wide range of public performing arts activities. In early spring 1982, the park's theater accidentally burned but it was rebuilt with funds from public donations and federal government loans. Harold Flacknoe photo; courtesy of National Park Service

142

An orchestra of more than 110 musicians, the Fairfax Symphony, conducted by William Hudson, was founded in 1956. Eighteen musicians met for the first rehearsal. Thirty years later, the orchestra presents a six-concert season series, including a performance at the Kennedy Center, a family holiday festival, and benefit concerts. It also maintains an educational program which takes groups of instrumentalists and a fifty-piece orchestra into the schools. In 1982, Virginia Governor Charles S. Robb described the Fairfax Symphony as one of the "community's most important assets" and "a musical showpiece for the entire state of Virginia."

Founded in 1962, the Fairfax Choral Society is made up of volunteer singers who audition annually and rehearse under a strict attendance policy. Over the years the chorus has performed with the Arlington, Fairfax, and National Symphonies, and on the stages of Constitution Hall, the Kennedy Center, and Wolf Trap's Filene Center. Under the direction of Robert E. McCord, the ninety-voice chorus presents four concerts each season. From the beginning, the Fairfax Choral Society has offered the community masterworks in choral literature, in several instances the first public performances of these works in Virginia.

Shown above are members of the Fairfax Symphony and the Fairfax Choral Society in concert at the National Presbyterian Church, Washington, D.C., in November 1982. Photograph by Jerome Breiter; courtesy of the Fairfax Choral Society

The rustic barns of Wolf Trap Park provide a marked contrast to the majestic and spacious outdoor pavilion of the Filene Center across the road in the only national park for the performing arts. "The Barns" have been modified and joined to form an acoustically perfect 350-seat theater and lounge area, and provide an intimate showcase for some of the finest entertainers in folk, country, bluegrass, jazz and classical music. The weathered buildings, each over 200 years old—one of German design (left) and one of English (right)—were found in Pennsylvania. They were disassembled and moved to the Wolf Trap Foundation site. Carefully reassembled by skilled craftsmen, The Barns theater was ready for performances by the winter of 1981. Varied programs have been offered ever since, usually between October and May. They have included such artists as Doc Watson, Judy Collins, Barbara Cook, the Charlie Byrd Trio, the Preservation Hall Jazz Band, the New Sousa Band, the Virginia Chamber Orchestra, Barter Theater, Beverly Sills, and Placido Domingo. Performing arts demonstrations are also offered here weekly during the school year by the Wolf Trap Institute for Early Learning Through the Arts to area pre-school children in Head Start programs. Courtesy of Wolf Trap Foundation

In performance at Wolf Trap Farm Park is the internationally known recording artist John Jackson from Fairfax Station. During the 1970s Jackson made several tours of foreign countries in cultural exchanges sponsored by the State Department, singing and playing folk songs and ethnic music. He is shown here (center) with dancer Malathi Ramji (left) and William Hoffnagle, Chairman of the Board of Supervisors (right) in a Fairfax County Family Night performance at Wolf Trap Farm in 1972. Fairfax County Department of Recreation photo; courtesy of Fairfax County Library Photographic Archive

Courtesy of Fairfax County Department of Recreation

Responding to the enthusiasm of its residents for opportunities to participate in the graphic and performing arts, Fairfax County offers activities sponsored by public and private sector organizations and the academic community. Illustrating the variety of these activities, these photographs show one of the periodic art shows on the Courthouse lawn by the County's Department of Recreation in 1967; a scene from George Mason University's Fall Dance Festival, December 1981; a performance by the Barter Theater, since 1946 the State Theater of Virginia, at the Harris Theater of George Mason University; and Green Spring Farm, owned by the Fairfax County Park Authority, headquarters of the Fairfax County Council of the Arts, and frequently used as a gallery for special exhibits.

Courtesy of McLean Providence Journal, *Fairfax County Library Photographic Archive*

Carl Zitzman photo; courtesy of George Mason University

Media General Cable's system has a capacity of 120 channels, more active than any other cable television system nationwide. Since 1983 its service has been available in Fairfax County, Fairfax City, Falls Church, Vienna, Herndon, and Clifton.

The government, schools and libraries are programming their own channels and the cable company produces a news program as well as local programming. There also are channels programmed by the Fairfax County Access Corporation and Fairfax Cable Association, a cooperative, which accommodate programs generated by citizen organizations. Mattox photo; courtesy of Media General Cable of Fairfax

In 1950 Northern Virginians seeking college or professional education had to look to Washington or suburban Maryland where six major universities and numerous professional schools were located. These schools had not been able to expand their facilities during the years of wartime shortages, however, and did not meet the new demand for education that came in the 1950s. Despite this evident need, it was not until 1964 that the Virginia General Assembly created a State Board for Technical Education. This cleared the way for establishment of the Northern Virginia Technical College in a rented warehouse at Bailey's Crossroads in 1965. From this beginning, the school in 1968 became Northern Virginia Community College, the first accredited member of Virginia's present Community College system. Currently the college offers programs at five campuses: Annandale, Alexandria, Manassas, Woodbridge, and Loudoun County. This photograph shows the College's Annandale Campus viewed from the Little River Turnpike. Bob Hoy photo; courtesy of Northern Virginia Community College

Plans for a community center for McLean evolved over several decades and several sites were considered before one was selected adjacent to the central park and library (near Dolley Madison Boulevard and Old Dominion Drive) at the center of the Greater McLean area. In 1970, voters in a special district covering most of Greater McLean approved an $800,000 bond issue for land acquisition and construction. The community center opened its doors in June 1975. In a memorandum of understanding between the Fairfax County Board of Supervisors

and the Governing Board of the Special District, responsibilities for maintenance and operation of the center were defined. A wide range of activities are carried on at the center, with special facilities for youth activities and senior citizen programs. Plans for expansion include

facilities for the performing arts and exhibition galleries and a hall of history featuring maps, pictures, and displays dealing with the historic heritage of the McLean area (McLean Community Center Handbook). Courtesy of McLean Community Center

A wide variety of special programs for senior citizens is coordinated by the Fairfax County Area Agency on Aging and the county's Department of Recreation. In this photograph, the Chairman of the Fairfax County Board of Supervisors, Jack Herrity (left), and Supervisor from Mason District, Thomas Davis, III (right), address an informational meeting on nutrition (Fairfax County Citizens Handbook). *Courtesy of Fairfax County Library Photographic Archive*

George Mason University opened in 1950 as an extension of the University of Virginia, and many hailed it as a step toward the realization of Thomas Jefferson's 1817 plan for a series of regional colleges each "within a day's ride" of the homes of those it was intended to serve. In 1957 the University's Board of Visitors authorized establishment at Bailey's Crossroads of a two-year branch college named George Mason College in honor of Fairfax County's famous patriot-statesman. In 1966 the college was elevated to university status by action of the General *Assembly and given a mandate for expansion into a major center of education, research, and service to the community. The search for a permanent campus site resulted in selection of a tract on the edge of Fairfax City in 1970. Steady expansion of this site and construction of facilities has continued since that time. Shown in this photograph is the campus' central library named in honor of Charles Fenwick of Arlington, who, as a member of the Virginia Senate, was an early leader in working for establishment of the university. Carl Zitzman photo; courtesy of George Mason University*

*A*s railroad service ceased on many of the short-haul lines in Northern Virginia, some of the abandoned rights-of-way were converted to other uses. Through the cooperation of the electric utility and the local governments, the Northern Virginia Regional Park Authority created a linear park on the right-of-way of the Washington and Old Dominion Railroad. Here, where it leaves Arlington and enters Falls Church, the park path accommodates a variety of activities. Richard Netherton photo

*T*he twelve miles of State Route 193 connecting Langley and Dranesville was in June 1974 officially designated as a Virginia Byway under legislation authorizing such action for roads traversing areas of particular scenic beauty, or historic, natural, or recreational significance. This two-lane road through rolling hills, woods, and open fields is on the location of a colonial era rolling road, later improved as the Georgetown-Leesburg Turnpike built in the 1830s. Today it is intended to preserve the opportunity for leisurely recreational motoring. It is the first of eleven official Virginia Byways (Virginia Outdoors). Richard Netherton photo

Fairfax County's wealth of historic sites and natural areas preserved for public enjoyment and education are, in many instances, the result of the generosity of the county's residents. An example of such a gift is Ellanor C. Lawrence County Park, a square mile of land at Centreville comprised of forests, fields, and streams. This park, possibly the most valuable gift ever donated to a local government in Virginia, contains several old houses and an old mill on Great Rocky Run, and in 1971 was valued at $4,960,000. The gift was made through the will of Mrs. Ellanor C. Lawrence, shown here. She was the wife of David Lawrence, publisher of U.S. News and World Report. *Courtesy of the Lawrence family and Fairfax County Library Photographic Archive*

The transportation links which connect Northern Virginia in an interrelated and dynamic region are shown here in an aerial view of Route 66 as it enters Fairfax County from Arlington County and the city of Falls Church. This photo looks east from the vicinity of the West Falls Church Metro Station (lower right corner), across the city of Falls Church (upper right corner) to the high-rise skyline of Rosslyn and the Potomac River (top center).

Construction of Route 66 inside the Beltway was the subject of lengthy controversy and litigation over its potential socio-economic and environmental impacts on the communities which it traverses. Designed as an expressway with divided roadways, separation of grades at intersections, and access only at interchanges, Route 66 also provides space for the Metro System's transit tracks in the highway median strip. The highway lanes of Route 66 inside the Beltway were opened to traffic in December 1982. The Metro trains in the median strip of Route 66 began operations to Fairfax County's stations at West Falls Church, Dunn Loring and Vienna in the summer of 1986. Scott Boatright photo, 1986; courtesy Fairfax County Police Department

Ice hockey below the Mason-Dixon line is no longer an impossible dream, as this action photo shows. The padded young contestants are at the Mount Vernon Sports Complex of the Fairfax County Park Authority, one of the most unusual publicly owned recreational facilities in the country. Situated in the eighty-seven acre Mount Vernon District Park, the indoor facility operates year-round and contains swimming pools and an indoor ice rink equipped to National Hockey League standards. In addition to hockey, the rink offers public skating and special events.
Photo courtesy of Fairfax County Park Authority

In July 1985, George Mason University added a major regional sports and entertainment facility with the opening of its 10,000 seat Patriot Center. The building, covering 162,000 square feet (approximately two acres), is of steel truss construction, and free of interior columns. Designed by the Richmond architectural firm of Corneal and Johnson, it was built at a cost of $16.7 million, and is managed by the Capital Centre organization. The Patriot Center houses such events as commencements, basketball and soccer games, trade shows, concerts and ice shows. Shown here is action on the basketball court as Georgetown University plays George Mason University. Carl Zitzman photo, courtesy of George Mason University

Outdoor recreation combining the best of water and shoreline facilities is offered at Pohick Bay Regional Park, a facility on the Potomac at Mason Neck owned by the Northern Virginia Regional Park Authority. Pohick, an Algonquin Indian word for "the water place," lives up to its name, for the developed recreation area merges into a marshland nature preserve where wildfowl (egrets, osprey, and bald eagle), deer, and beaver abound. Photo courtesy of Northern Virginia Regional Park Authority

Christian Adolph "Sonny" Jurgensen, of Fairfax County and the Football Hall of Fame, symbolizes the popularity of sports throughout Northern Virginia. In his career as quarterback for the Washington Redskins from 1964 to 1975, he established three National Football League and Redskin all-time passing records and was awarded All-Pro honors five times. Since retiring from the Redskins in 1975, Jurgensen has served as a member of the WDVM-TV sports staff and as a sports analyst for the CBS television network. Courtesy of WDVM-TV

Clowns, balloons and exhibits are part of the festivities in mid-June when the Fairfax Fair is held on the campus of George Mason University. County fairs have been held in Fairfax since the mid-eighteenth century when Alexandria was the county seat. The modern county fair concept was reactivated in 1982 to revive overall community spirit. Traditional aspects of arts, crafts, farming and home-making are combined in this annual event with a host of modern activities and high-tech exhibits, funded by the business community and the county government. Marty Kaplan photo, 1985; courtesy Kaplan Studio, McLean, Virginia

Olympic gold medalist Melissa Belote learned to swim at the age of three in a community swimming pool in Springfield. Her first competition was in the inter-community swimming pool leagues of Fairfax County. From this start, she went on to win three gold medals swimming backstroke in the 1972 Olympic Games in Munich, Germany. Courtesy of Fairfax County Library Photographic Archive

A master of the casting art, Clifford Netherton of Great Falls, demonstrates flycasting as he has taught it to thousands of fishing enthusiasts in a twenty-five year career as teacher, coach, and consultant. He illustrates the revival of interest in outdoor recreation that has accompanied the urbanization of Fairfax County and the strong public support that developed in the 1960s and 1970s for conservation of open space and natural areas in Northern Virginia. Traveling widely as president of the American Casting Association and an organizer of the International Casting Federation, Netherton pioneered in training instructors and writing instruction materials. Three times a participant in the World Casting Championship, he was elected to the Casting Hall of Fame in 1973. Courtesy of Fairfax County Library Photographic Archive

Jubilantly holding their 1983 National High School Rugby Championship Trophy, Ivan Lopez-Munoz (left) and David MacLaury (right), co-captains of the Langley Rugby Club, celebrate with their teammates. The team was organized in 1974 with fifteen boys, only one of whom knew how to play the game. Learning as they played and growing with new recruits, the team has been sponsored since 1979 by McLean Youth, Inc. After winning three East Coast championships, the Langley Rugby Club in 1983 won the national championship by a decisive 13-9 victory over the West Coast champions, San Mateo Serra Rugby Club. The Langley team members buy their own equipment and are coached by community volunteers, and claim that pride and teamwork are their secrets of success. Adrian Carpenter photo, courtesy of Brooks Lowery

Stepping out briskly in formation, the Fairfax City Regional Library Precision Book Cart Drill Team, shown in action here, has become a popular feature of Fairfax County parades. The team's skill in maneuvering its library book carts through colorful and complex patterns has earned it trophies whenever it has marched. Fairfax County's Public Library system also has consistently circulated more books and other library materials than any other library system in the South. Courtesy of Fairfax County Public Library

Reston residents since 1967, Carol and Tom Deakin helped begin the recreated First Virginia Regiment of the Continental Line in 1975 as part of Fairfax County's celebration of the nation's Bicentennial. Active throughout the Bicentennial years in living history with the regiment, which was first commanded by Virginia's Patrick Henry, the Deakins together, at the invitation of Virginia and National Park Service authorities, in 1976 proposed the plan to observe the Bicentennial of the Victory at Yorktown. The couple gathered 4,000 living history buffs to portray Revolutionary War soldiers and their camp followers at the Yorktown event in 1981. Some 120 recreated Revolutionary War units, commanded by the Deakins, representing American, French, British and Hessian forces passed in review before the presidents of the United States and France at the Yorktown battlefield site. Hernandez photo, courtesy of Tom and Carol Deakin

With wig and knee breeches, John Victor of Vienna explains the uses of one of the herb medicines from his eighteenth-century medicine chest. Victor's interest in doctors and medical practice in colonial times began when he served as Commanding Officer of the First Virginia Regiment for the bicentennial celebration in 1976, and since that time he has continued it at George Mason University as a second career in lecturing, writing, demonstrating, and exhibiting facets of British and American medical practice of the eighteenth century. Myrna Garza Miller photo; courtesy of George Mason University

The largest dog in Fairfax County is Nipper, a fifteen foot fiberglass replica of the famous terrier who for almost half a century was part of the trademark of RCA Victor phonograph records. Made in 1950 as a rooftop advertising display for a Baltimore distributor, Nipper and his Victrola phonograph were displayed by their owner until the business was relocated in 1975. At that point Jim Wells of Fairfax was able to buy Nipper and his Victrola for one dollar. Removed to Wells' front yard on Route 29-211 one mile east of Fairfax City, Nipper has become not only the largest dog in Fairfax County but also the most famous one (Fairfax Globe). Tuan Tran photo for NAPCO, Inc.

By 1950, the rising tide of new residents in Fairfax County faced a critical need for some forum in which to explore common problems, seek solutions, and coordinate civic activities. At the neighborhood level, community citizens associations grew up almost spontaneously in response to this need; and at the county level, the Fairfax County Federation of Citizens Associations was formed in 1945.

Shown in the photograph taken at the 1982 Federation of Citizens Annual Awards Dinner are Virginia Governor Charles Robb and Lilla D. McC. Richards, president of the Federation. This marked the first occasion on which a governor had been keynote speaker at a Fairfax Federation annual award ceremony. *Courtesy of Fairfax County Federation of Citizens Associations*

"*A funny looking ship,*" something like a preying mantis ready to pounce, was what watchers on the shore said about the USS Fairfax County as she made her way up-river toward the Custom House dock in July 1972 on her first visit to Alexandria. Actually, she was one of the new fast tank landing ships—522 feet long and displacing 8,000 tons—built to replace the bulky sluggish LSTs that carried tanks, trucks, and troops to the beaches in World War II and Korea. Capable of cruising at twenty knots, she could keep up with a fast convoy and the huge derrick in her bow increased her

In January 1982, Charles Robb of McLean was inaugurated as the sixty-fourth Governor of the Commonwealth of Virginia and was sworn in by Chief Justice of the Virginia Supreme Court of Appeals Harry Carrico, a lifelong resident and distinguished attorney of Fairfax County. As the oath of office was being given, a moment of merriment ensued when the Chief Justice asked the

Governor-elect to raise his right hand and to place his right hand on the Bible being held by Lynda Bird Johnson Robb. As they corrected the confusing instructions, the Governor-elect quipped, "I think we should have had more rehearsal of this part, Mr. Chief Justice." *Courtesy of Office of the Governor, Commonwealth of Virginia*

efficiency in landing and taking on her cargo. The USS Fairfax County, commissioned in 1970, was the latest in a long series of ships in English and American history to bear the Fairfax name. The USS Fairfax County carried on board a plaque of the county seal pre-

sented to its commanding officer at her commissioning by Captain Carl Porter, representing Fairfax County (Washington Post). *Courtesy of Fairfax County Library Photographic Archive*

J. Hamilton Lambert, County Executive

The Builders' House 1985 on Bennington Woods Road in Reston's North Point Village is shown at the fifty-four hour point in the seventy-two hour construction project. Area home builders planned and coordinated the job for six months before the race began on September 4, 1985. As many as 2,000 builders, heavy equipment operators, carpenters, masons, plumbers, electricians, interior decorators and landscapers donated time, talent and materials to erect the 5,000 square foot structure in three days. It was raffled off to provide over one million dollars to three designated Northern Virginia charities—the Paul Anderson Youth Home, Haven of Northern Virginia, and Hartwood Home. The successful project was sponsored by the Outreach Committee, composed of wives of over 100 members of the Northern Virginia Builders Association. The winner of the raffle was William L. Oram. Courtesy of Peter L. McCandless

In January 1986, Vivian Watts of Annandale was sworn in as Secretary of Transportation and Public Safety in the cabinet of Governor Gerald Baliles. Mrs. Watts is the first woman to serve in this office, which oversees operation of the Commonwealth's 53,000 mile highway system; 3,700 miles of railroads; 81 airports; the Port Authority of Hampton Roads; and the river ports of Alexandria, Hopewell and Richmond. In addition, she heads the state's police and military forces, correctional facilities, motor vehicle department, and fire programs.

As a member of the Virginia House of Delegates for the 39th District from 1981 to 1985, Mrs. Watts became an acknowledged leader in working to modernize and expand the transportation systems serving the needs of Fairfax County as the hub of rapidly-growing Northern Virginia. Courtesy of the Office of the Governor of Virginia

The Board of Supervisors is the administrative body of Fairfax County's government. Elected in 1984 and sworn in by Circuit Court Clerk Warren E. Barry, were Audrey Moore, Annandale District; Sandra Duckworth, Mount Vernon District; James M. Scott, Providence District; John F. Herrity, Chairman, elected at-large; Martha V. Pennino, Centreville District; Thomas M. Davis, III, Mason District; Nancy K. Falck, Dranesville District; Elaine McConnell, Springfield District; and Joseph Alexander, Lee District. Mrs. Duckworth moved from the area in 1984, and T. Farrell Egge was elected to take her place. Sheriff Wayne M. Huggins stands behind Mr. Barry and Mrs. Moore, and Commonwealth's Attorney Robert Horan stands to the far left, next to the flag. Courtesy Fairfax County Office of Public Affairs

The Falls Church was first constructed of weather board in 1733. By 1763 wear and tear had taken their toll and a committee of vestrymen, which included George Washington, recommended that the church be replaced rather than repaired. The year after Fairfax Parish was separated from Truro Parish in 1765, the Fairfax vestry ordered that a new brick church was to be built "where the old church stands."

After the disestablishment of the state church (Anglican) by the legislature in 1784, a new denomination of the Protes-

tant Episcopal Church of Virginia was formed that included The Falls Church. When the building fell into a ruinous condition in the early 1800s, Captain Henry Fairfax of Ash Grove, son of Thomas Ninth Baron Fairfax of Cameron, saw to it that the necessary repairs were made in order to preserve the old church.

The village of Falls Church was caught between the two opposing armies during the Civil War as was much of Fairfax County. Confederate troops were stationed in the church in 1861; Union troops later used it as a hospital, then tore

up the floor boards and used the church for a stable. After the war, the U.S. government appropriated money for needed repairs.

Since World War II, the church congregation has grown like the area surrounding the old landmark, which has itself been enlarged. The Falls Church Day School has been established, and the church's bicentennial history was written from the old vestry book records and published in 1969 (Alves, Near the Falls). Courtesy of Library of Congress

Towns and Cities: Places Apart

In the earliest settlement of the land which now is Fairfax County, the aboriginal Indians, and later the European settlers, chose sites near pure water supplies and river transportation for their villages and towns. This can still be seen in the location of the towns and cities which have survived. Where the land has not been disturbed by cultivation or building, it still yields ancient Indian and colonial artifacts to the dedicated searcher.

None of the Indian towns survive and only one of the early towns established by Scots merchants and English landowners still exists. Alexandria, the first town to be established within the county's borders, in 1749, has continued its existence on the deep water of the Potomac River. Colchester, established as a town in 1753 for tobacco and other commerce, is now merely a residential community. Its location on the north bank of the Occoquan River proved to be impractical. Unwise agricultural practices led to major erosion of lands upstream, the river silted up, and it was no longer navigable by ocean-going vessels even in colonial times.

Many other towns were created only on paper, or else were founded but never quite lived up to expectations. These included Philee, 1772; Matildaville, 1790; Centreville, 1792; South Haven, 1798; Turberville, 1798; Dranesville, 1840; and Wiehle, 1898 (Virginia *Acts of Assembly*).

All of the existing towns and cities, except for Alexandria were incorporated after the Civil War, even Fairfax, which had first been incorporated as the Town of Providence. In each case, since all were on major transportation arteries, the community was included in a postal district prior to being incorporated as a town.

Fairfax County presently operates under the urban county form of government, administered by a board of supervisors elected from each of the eight magisterial districts, plus a chairman elected at-large. A county executive serves at the pleasure of the board. Virginia statutes presently prohibit the formation of new towns and cities within urban county borders. This is the reason the "new town" of Reston is actually an unincorporated community within the county; the Centreville District supervisor represents its interests on the county board level.

In the Commonwealth of Virginia, town residents pay local taxes twice, to their town government and to the county as well; city dwellers pay local taxes to the city government only. In many cases, the cities contract with the county to provide specified educational, social, and legal services. Yet in their traditions and lifestyles all of the towns and cities that have survived are places apart from the county, and each retains something of the early influences that shaped

the county's growth.

Herndon and Clifton proudly nourish their traditions as railroad towns. Falls Church retains a quiet residential quality that was so highly valued by those who settled there after the Civil War that it was described as a "transplanted New England village." Vienna was also influenced by transplanted New Englanders after the Civil War, but its present style is characterized by the vitality that goes with being the largest town in Virginia. Fairfax City, the most recent place to attain separate status, is evolving a style that blends the traditions of the county's historic seat of government with the lively influence of nearby George Mason University. And finally, Reston, although not legally a separate municipality, is well along in developing its own unique style based on modern-day themes and already is a place apart in its pride and traditions.

Joseph E. Willard was the only son of Antonia Ford and Joseph Willard. He was born in 1863 and later was graduated from Episcopal High School, Virginia Military Institute, and the University of Virginia Law School. In 1893 he was elected to the Virginia House of Delegates, where he served four terms. He served in the Spanish-American War and in 1901 was elected lieutenant governor of Virginia.

Willard's home in Fairfax, Layton Hall, was a showplace, and his wealth as a member of the Willard Hotel family enabled him to participate actively in local affairs and to be acquainted with important national and international figures.

President Woodrow Wilson appointed Willard Minister to Spain from 1913 to 1921. It was in Madrid that his daughter Belle was married to Kermit Roosevelt, son of Theodore Roosevelt. Willard's daughter Elizabeth married the son of the fifth Earl of Carnavon, the Egyptologist who financed Howard Carter's successful expedition to find the tomb of King Tutankhamen. Joseph Willard died in 1924 (Eskew, Willards). Fairfax County Courthouse portrait

Earp's Ordinary, Fairfax City's oldest remaining residence, was constructed early in the nineteenth century after the Town of Providence was established on land formerly owned by Richard Ratcliffe.

For some time after 1820, it was operated as a post station and stagecoach stop by owners Gordon and Robert Allison. It fell into disrepair during the Civil War and after, and was due to be demolished in 1923 when Dr. Kate

Waller Barrett of Alexandria purchased it. At the time, it was thought to be the old Earp's Ordinary although no documentation has been found. Dr. Barrett's daughter, Mrs. Charles Pozer, a columnist for the Washington Post, *lived in the house for many years and left it to the City upon her death in 1981. The building is listed on the Virginia Historic Landmarks Register. William Edmund Barrett photo*

Fairfax City

The Fairfax County Courthouse location was moved from Alexandria in 1800 because of the formation of the Federal District of Columbia which originally included Alexandria. A site was selected in the approximate center of the county where the old Ox Road, between Colchester and the Frying Pan copper mines (Route 123) crossed the Little River Turnpike (Route 236), which was a transportation link between Alexandria, Aldie in Loudoun County, and the Shenandoah Valley.

A postal district by the name of Fairfax Court House was designated on April 7, 1802, with John Ratcliffe as postmaster. In 1805, the Virginia Assembly approved the incorporation of fourteen acres of land surrounding the courthouse owned by Richard Ratcliffe as the Town of Providence (Lisbeth, "Post Offices"; Virginia *Acts of Assembly*).

During the Civil War, the town was occupied by Confederate forces in 1861. Then, after the Second Battle of Manassas in 1862, the Confederates moved southward and Union troops occupied the town until the close of the conflict in 1865.

In 1875, the name of the Town of Providence was changed to Fairfax by the Virginia Assembly, although it had customarily been called Fairfax Court House since the postal designation in 1802. Fairfax was incorporated as a city in 1961.

The county's courthouse complex, including the old and new courthouses, the old and new jails, and the Massey office building, form a county enclave within the city's boundaries.

The city's total land area is six square miles; the 1980 population count was 19,390.

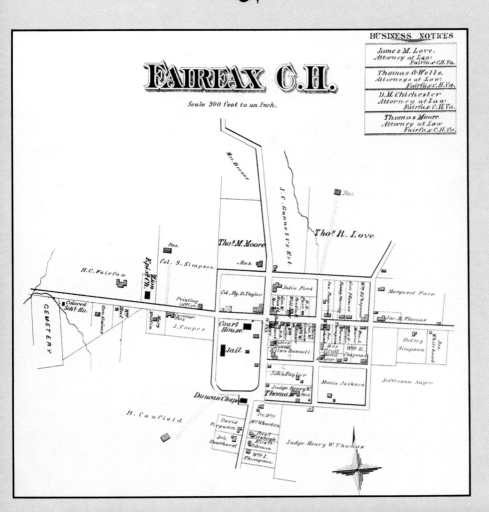

Map of Fairfax Court House from Hopkins' Atlas, *1878*

*R*obert Walton Moore was a direct descendant of colonial Baptist preacher Jeremiah Moore. He was born in 1859 and was educated at Episcopal High School and at the University of Virginia, where he studied law. He served as a state senator from 1887 to 1890 and was a U.S. Congressman from 1919 to 1931.

Moore acted as counsel in cases before a number of government agencies for over twenty years. A good friend of Cordell Hull, he was appointed Assistant Secretary of State in 1933 by President Franklin D. Roosevelt and worked at the State Department until his death in 1941. In 1981, his daughter, Mrs. F. Shield McCandlish, Sr., deeded his home on Chain Bridge Road across from the post office to the City of Fairfax for community use. Fairfax County Courthouse portrait

*T*he Willcoxen Tavern was built early in the nineteenth century by Rezin Willcoxen who had moved to Fairfax County from Maryland. It was located on the corner, across Little River Turnpike from the old county courthouse, where the First and Merchants Bank now stands. Here lawyers had offices, visitors and litigants boarded, and the first telephone in Fairfax was installed in 1887.

Through the years, it was operated as a hotel under several different names and proprietors until 1932 when the building was demolished, replaced by the National Bank of Fairfax. Mr. and Mrs. Francis Pickens Miller purchased the old bricks, mantels, doors, and hardware, and built Pickens Hill, now the administration building for the Flint Hill Private School complex on Chain Bridge Road in Oakton (Rust, Fairfax). Helen Hill Miller photo, 1932; courtesy of Fairfax County Library Photographic Archive

*F*airfax City Hall was built in a colonial style in 1962 to house the administrative offices, courtrooms, and police department of the newly created city. An outdoor brick amphitheater has been built for summer band and orchestra concerts and holiday celebrations, programs, and parades. Tom Welle photo; courtesy of City of Fairfax

The Fairfax baseball team, shown about 1910, was part of a popular national movement which found active teams in almost every little hamlet in the county. Feelings often ran high; more than one game was called by the umpires because of fighting among the players. Transportation used by the teams in this period was often the nearest railroad, and time schedules had to be accommodated. There is on record at least one game in nearby Clifton having been called "on account of train." Courtesy of Fairfax County Library Photographic Archive

Fairfax High School and community center was constructed on a forty-eight acre tract under a bond issue approved by the city voters. It was the most modern community high school in the mid-Atlantic region when it was completed in 1972.

The library, shown here, the instructional space, the rooftop greenhouse, the vocational training shops, the 5,000-seat field house, the athletic and health areas, and the 800-seat cafeteria provide facilities and amenities utilized by both the city's student population, grades nine through twelve, and adults, including senior citizens, after school hours.

The 1,200-seat auditorium, with orchestra pit and dressing room, provides space for 150 rehearsals and performances by area community groups each year. Because so many performing arts programs have been presented here, Fairfax High has proudly been called "the Kennedy Center of Northern Virginia." Bernie Boston photo, 1976

Falls Church

Although strong tradition places a house—Big Chimneys—in Falls Church as early as 1699, the first documented record of an actual building on the future site of the city appeared in the minutes of the Truro Parish Vestry Book in 1733. In that year, a church was proposed to be built "at the Cross Roads near Michael Reagans" (Alves, *Near the Falls*). It was soon thereafter named after the Little Falls in the Potomac River several miles away, which, in the early colonial period of vast, unoccupied distances, seemed to provide a geographic identity close by.

A settlement gradually grew up around the crossroads and the church, and in 1849, a Falls Church postal district was established with Charles H. Upton of Upton's Hill the first postmaster (Lisbeth, "Post Offices," *Yearbook*).

The Alexandria, Loudoun and Hampshire Railroad was built through the community in 1858. It furnished passenger and freight service, except for the Civil War period, until 1968 (Harwood, *Rails*). Known as the Washington and Old Dominion Railroad when it finally went out of business, the right-of-way was sold to the Virginia Electric and Power Company for transmission lines, and the Northern Virginia Regional Park Authority purchased part of the property for a linear park bike, hike, and riding trail.

After the disruption of the Civil War, the area began to put itself back together again, and in 1875 a movement led by Joseph Riley of Cherry Hill led to the incorporation of the town. Ten years later, a Village Improvement Society was established, patterned after the Laurel Hill Society of Stockbridge, Massachusetts. Under the new organization's sponsorship, the first official observance of Arbor Day in Virginia was held in Falls Church in 1892.

The advent of improved communication and transportation—the telephone, the electric trolley commuter line, automobiles, and electricity—made Falls Church a pleasant place in which government employees could live and easily get back and forth to work. Their numbers grew through the First and Second World Wars and the time between.

Falls Church almost doubled its population in the eight years after 1940, and in 1948, the town successfully applied to the state legislature for city status separating it from Fairfax County. It is two square miles in area and the 1980 U.S. Census found the population to be 9,515.

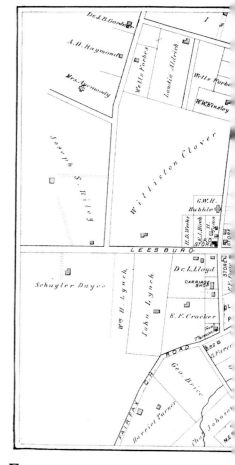

Falls Church map from Hopkins' Atlas, *1878*

The farm land was possibly occupied as early as 1753, but the present Cherry Hill house was probably not built until about 1840. Joseph S. Riley, an uncle of poet James Whitcomb Riley, acquired eighty acres of property and the house in 1870 and it was in family ownership until his son, Joseph Harvey Riley, a noted ornithologist and author, died in 1941. He left the estate to the University of Virginia.

When the city council decided they wanted to build a new city hall on the Cherry Hill estate, City Manager Harry Wells was successful in negotiating the purchase from the University of Virginia.

The corn crib, well house, necessary (privy), barn, and house itself have been restored and are maintained by the city. The Friends of Cherry Hill Foundation assists with periodic acquisitions of authentic furnishings of the 1840-1850 period and manages a docent program with guides for school tours and visitors on occasions when the house is open to the public (Wrenn, Cherry Hill). Courtesy of Falls Church Historical Commission

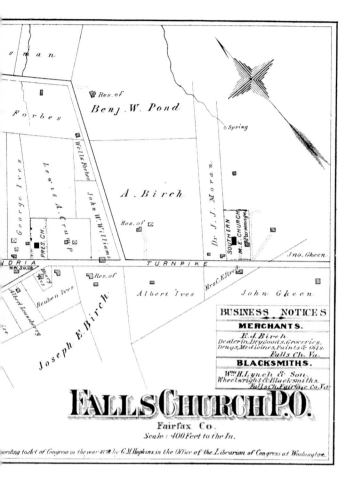

BUSINESS NOTICES
MERCHANTS.
E.J.Birch.
Dealer in Dry Goods, Groceries,
Drugs, Medicines, Paints & Oils.
Falls Ch. Va.
BLACKSMITHS.
Wm.H.Lynch & Son.
Wheelwright & Blacksmiths.
Falls Ch. Fairfax co.Va.

FALLS CHURCH P.O.
Fairfax Co.
Scale : 400 Feet to the In.

A movement led by Joseph Riley and others resulted in the incorporation of Falls Church as a town in 1875. Riley went to Richmond to lobby the act through the legislature partly because of "the deplorable conditions in the village due to the unregulated sale of drink. Apparently there was so much loafing and drinking that ladies could not walk about without embarrassment." (Steadman, Falls Church).

Riley owned a bookstore on Seventh Street in Washington and an export business in Richmond. He moved to Cherry Hill in 1873, was the first chairman of the Falls Church School Board, was elected to the Town Council in 1876, and also served as a magistrate and justice of the peace. Portrait courtesy of Melvin L. Steadman

*A*n old log school house, various churches, and several homes were used as schools in Falls Church before the Jefferson Institute, a solid three-story brick building, was completed by Richard Ratcliffe Farr in 1882. It was located facing East Broad Street on the hill behind present-day Donald Frady Park next to Cherry Street, and served as a school until 1956 at which time the students were moved to the newly opened Mount Daniel Elementary School. The picture was taken in 1891, the same year a tornado whipped through town while school was in session and did no more damage than to take off the roof. Jefferson was demolished in 1958.

Madison School was built on North Washington Street at Great Falls Street in 1926 of native stone with brick facings and was demolished in 1980. Oak Street School, now Thomas Jefferson Elementary, was opened in 1948 and George Mason Junior-Senior High in 1952. Courtesy of Melvin L. Steadman

163

Frederick Foote, Sr., of part Indian and part Negro ancestry, was born on Ravensworth plantation in 1800. With earnings from his labors on the building of the Chesapeake and Ohio Canal, he purchased over forty acres of land on the present site of Seven Corners Shopping Center, in 1864. The land was sold by his heirs for development in the 1950s.

His son, Frederick Forrest Foote, Jr., shown here, was a shoemaker and merchant who owned a large general store on the southeast corner of Broad and Washington streets. He was a highly respected member of the Falls Church community and served on the Town Council from 1880 to 1889 (Steadman, Falls Church). Courtesy of Melvin L. Steadman

The Falls Church Bakery, shown here about 1900, was owned by George L. Erwin, second from right. An advertisement in 1904 offered pies, cakes, and homemade bread. Free deliveries were made daily "at all residences in Falls Church, Vienna, Dunnloring, Lewinsville, Langley, Ballston, Baileys X Roads, Halls Hill and Merrifield."

At this period in the history of Falls Church, there were many other businesses including general merchants, confectioners, druggists, florists, coach and wagon builders, furniture dealers, dentists, and doctors within the town boundaries, Brown's Hardware has remained in business through the years to the present, celebrating their 100th anniversary in 1983. (Wrenn, Falls Church). Courtesy of Falls Church Historical Commission

The First Congregational Church of Falls Church was organized in 1875 and the congregation built this edifice in 1879. Because of gradual loss of membership, the church was abandoned in 1910.

Since that time, the building has had many uses. It has at various times served as a public school, a library, a recreation and community center, a town hall, police station, and an office building.

The Woman's Club of Falls Church purchased the structure in 1961 for its headquarters, did extensive renovation, and now makes it available for community

meetings (Steadman, Falls Church).

The old town water tower shown behind it is no more. It was taken down in 1979 along with the large star on top which was always lighted for the Christmas holiday season. Quentin Porter photo, 1949; courtesy of Fairfax County Library Photographic Archive

Dr. Louis E. Gott served with the first group of councilmen when Falls Church became an incorporated town in 1875. He was born in Washington, D.C., in 1838, attended Episcopal High School in Alexandria, and was graduated from the University of Maryland in 1861. He is shown here on the porch of his home in Falls Church in 1910 with his daughter Alys. The horse and buggy are hitched up in the side yard.

Dr. Gott died in 1916 and a tombstone

in The Falls Church graveyard was erected as a "tribute of love from his friends." It reads in part: "For four years he was a surgeon in the army of the Confederate States and for fifty-one years he practiced medicine in this vicinity, skillful, loyal, charitable, brave, he was a noble example of the COUNTRY DOCTOR" (Steadman, Falls Church). Photo from John Gott; courtesy of Virginia State Library

Miss Mattie Gundry came from Ohio and Maryland in 1893 to open up the Virginia Training School, an institution for mentally retarded children. It was the only one of its kind in the South and gradually became the second largest in the United States.

Miss Gundry was very active in all aspects of life in Falls Church. She was an active member of The Falls Church, was appointed a director of the Falls Church Bank in 1910, and was the first woman to be elected to and serve on the Town Council.

In 1920, she and Miss Willie May Darby bought Shadow Lawn (Whitehall) on Little Falls Street and operated it as a sanitarium. She also continued with the training school until her death in 1947 (Steadman, Falls Church). Porter photo, 1946; courtesy of Falls Church Historical Commission

The development of Falls Church at the turn of the century following the arrival of the electric trolley in the 1890s was largely to the credit of pharmacist Merton E. Church. He was involved in promotion of the electric railroad, the electric light company, telephone service, and he also edited the Falls Church Monitor newspaper.

One of his promotional appeals welcomed "the jaded fathers and mothers from the city to the place where children may enjoy life with nature, where the climate, conducive to refreshing sleep, soothes tired nerves and makes life to such again buoyant with youthful hopes and joys (Reed, Fairfax County). Courtesy of Melvin L. Steadman

"*Uncle Pete*" *Gillam was Falls Church's first garbage collector, beginning in 1890. He is shown here in front of Brown's Hardware Store with his ox cart. He was still on the job when the Thurber family lived in town, 1901-1902.*

In a letter to Mrs. Frank Acosta in 1958, James Thurber described him: "Our garbage was collected by an ancient white haired negro, not more than five feet tall, whose two-wheeled ox cart was pulled by a brace of oxen. His appearance never failed to enchant us boys, for he was not only out of the South, but out of the past, even out of fiction, as remarkable as old Uncle Tom himself" (Wrenn, Falls Church). Courtesy of Melvin L. Steadman

The Falls Church Community Center was built in 1968 after extensive study and planning by a committee advisory to the City Council. It is operated by the city's Parks and Recreation Department with a year-round recreational program suitable for all ages and interests. School grounds and buildings, including George Mason Junior-Senior High School, are also utilized for programs, as are eight city parks, a bike trail, Cherry Hill, and the Senior Center at the Gage House. Part of the community center is used as a polling place for local, state, and national elections.

The city also contributes on a per capita basis to the operation of the Northern Virginia Regional Park Authority so that all residents may use its park and recreational facilities. Richard Netherton photo

Edwin Bancroft Henderson was, throughout his long and productive adult life, engaged in the struggle for equality and justice under the law for black citizens. He repeatedly spoke out when it was dangerous and unpopular to do so.

Born in Washington, D.C., he was graduated from Howard and Columbia universities and attended summer courses at Harvard. He was a physical training teacher and basketball coach in the Washington public schools. In 1910 he and his wife, Mary Ellen, moved to Falls Church where his parents and grandmother lived. His wife became a teacher at the James Lee Elementary School and later its principal.

The couple bought an acre of property where the old log tobacco Falls Warehouse was said once to have stood and built on it a house where they raised their two sons (Steadman, Falls Church).

Henderson wrote two books. The Negro in Sports was published in 1939,

and The Black Athlete: Emergence and Arrival was published in 1970 as a volume in a series prepared by the Association for Negro Life and History.

When asked to appear before a committee hearing in Richmond concerned with the pending so-called anti-NAACP bills, Henderson was asked his race. He answered: "This calls for some consideration. One of my great grandfathers was an Indian. My father's father was a Portuguese and my mother's father was one of the highly respected citizens of Williamsburg, Virginia. Her mother was this gentleman's slave. Now, what race should I subscribe to?"

Henderson was optimistic and had faith that if whites and blacks could work and play together, the black man would "learn to know his brother better" and they could then live in harmony (Netherton, Fairfax Chronicles). Harris & Ewing photo; courtesy of Falls Church Historical Commission

Tallwood was built in 1870 for John Gheen, a butcher and farmer who had moved to Falls Church from Pennsylvania. It was surrounded by ninety-five acres of farm land and passed through a number of hands over the years. It was purchased in 1938 by Dr. Milton Eisenhower and his wife, Helen Eakin Eisenhower. During the five years they owned it, Major and Mrs. Dwight D. Eisenhower, Dr. Eisenhower's brother and sister-in-law, were frequent visitors. When World War II began, General Eisenhower stayed at Tallwood for a few months while waiting for his family to join him. He was working eighteen-hour days at the time and later wrote: "I cannot remember ever seeing their house in daylight during all the months I served in Washington" (Douglas, Falls Church); Netherton, Fairfax County).

Architectural historian Russell Wright gave Tallwood the highest rating possible on his 1969 inventory of Falls Church structures. William Edmund Barrett photo

The first unit of the present Falls Church City Hall was completed in 1957 following the purchase of the Riley's Cherry Hill tract from the University of Virginia. In 1983 a wing was added to the building as shown here. Surrounding the City Hall is a 14.7-acre park in which are located the community center, senior center, tennis and basketball courts, play and picnic areas, gardens, and the restored farm house and outbuildings of Cherry Hill.

By preserving Cherry Hill and its park as the city's historic and civic center, the city council has succeeded in achieving a goal set in a consultant's study in 1973:

If the City of Falls Church can preserve Cherry Hill in such a way that it becomes a useful part of the modern community, it will have made a substantial contribution to the understanding of American architectural history, as well as saving a significant monument of its own heritage (Dickey, "Restoration of Cherry Hill").

Barbara Gordon photo, courtesy city of Falls Church

The Falls Church Library was first established in 1899, sponsored by the Woman's Club of Falls Church. The modest collection of books was stored in a number of different public and commercial buildings until the colonial-style brick structure on North Virginia Avenue was opened in 1958. The lot on which it was built, once part of the Cherry Hill estate, was given to the city by Miss Elizabeth Morgan Styles and her brother, Francis H. Styles, both grandchildren of Joseph S. Riley. The local history collection was enriched by a gift of books from the Riley estate by Mrs. Charles Gage, one of Joseph S. Riley's daughters (Steadman, Falls Church). David Netherton photo

The Falls Church Senior Center was dedicated in June 1982 in a handsome two-story white frame house situated in Cherry Hill Park. The building houses a variety of educational, recreational, social service, and health activities for senior citizens, and a two-room gallery for educational exhibits on local history by the Falls Church Historical Commission. The house was built in 1909, and for the next sixty years was the residence of Charles and Maude Gage. Both of the Gages had careers in Federal service. Charles Gage became a world authority on tobacco production, and, in local affairs, he served on the Town Council and various boards and commissions.

The Gages called their home Poverty Pines in honor of the Virginia field pines that sprang up on land abandoned after the Civil War and later grew to provide sources of fuel and timber for Northern Virginia. The City of Falls Church acquired the house in 1974 for use as the city's Senior Center. Ross Netherton photo

Herndon

Captain William Lewis Herndon was a Virginia sea captain who went down with his ship, the *Central America,* off Cape Hatteras in a storm in 1857, after directing passengers and crew into lifeboats. A survivor is said to have told this story at a meeting called to choose a name for the new postal district. The village fathers decided to honor the dead hero and the Herndon post office was established July 13, 1858, with William W. Hollingsworth as postmaster (Lisbeth, "Post Offices").

The railroad which was built to the town in 1859 has been known by several names. It was first the Alexandria, Loudoun and Hampshire, then the Washington and Ohio, later the Southern Railway, and finally, the Washington and Old Dominion Railroad. It ran through the center of town providing a means of transporting dairy and other agricultural products from the Herndon area to the Washington and Baltimore markets. Supplies and manufactured goods were brought from those cities to the rural area.

Since the early 1960s, the proximity to Dulles International Airport and the "new town" of Reston have exerted strong influences for change on the formerly remote rural town.

The town was incorporated in 1879, using the post office name. It has an area of four and one-quarter square miles and a 1980 population count of 11,449.

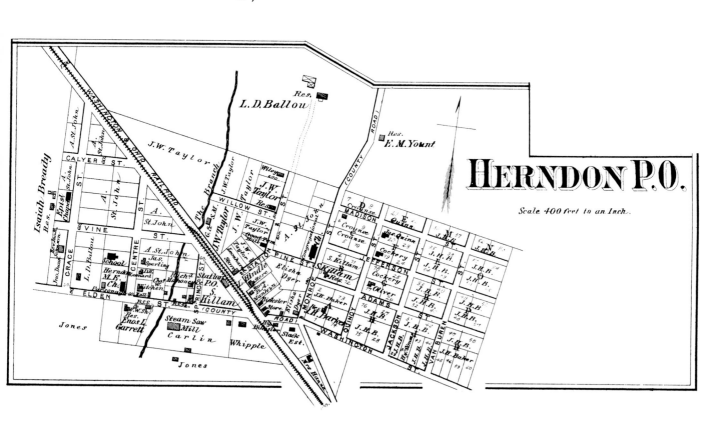

Map of Herndon from Hopkins' Atlas, 1878

William Lewis Herndon was directed in the 1840s by Matthew Fontaine Maury, Superintendent of the U.S. Department of Charts and Instruments, to explore the Amazon River for its entire length. After the mission was accomplished, Herndon and his assistant, Lardner Gibbon, collaborated on a two-volume scholarly work, written in a literary style, called Exploration of the Valley of the Amazon, *a report that Mark Twain later said inspired him to write* Life on the Mississippi *(Heite, "Scientist on the Bridge").*

Herndon's portrait may be seen at the depot museum, along with memorabilia from his ill-fated ship, the Central America, *and from the U.S.S.* Herndon. *The members of the crew of the* Herndon *recently presented the Town of Herndon with two flags that had been flown on shipboard, one in the Normandy invasion, and one in the Sicily invasion, as well as a Japanese flag from the surrender ceremony, part of which was held on the* Herndon. *Portrait courtesy of Virginia State Library*

The first public school building was erected in Herndon in 1869. Most of the early settlers were northerners who were used to the New England town-supported public education system. A new public school was built on Locust Street in 1910, at the present site of the Herndon Intermediate School. Several elementary and high schools have been built in different locations since then.

Just before the town was incorporated in 1879, a widowed first cousin of General Robert E. Lee came to Herndon to live, bringing her son and four daughters. Mrs. Robert Allen Castleman established the Herndon Seminary,

shown here, at 106 Grace Street. Her daughters, the Misses Mary, Lula, Ida, and Virginia Castleman continued the school after their mother died, until the mid-1920s. Their brother, the Reverend Allen Castleman, served as Episcopal minister at The Falls Church from 1917 to 1931.

Virginia Castleman left a literary legacy to Herndon in her detailed recording of the charming nineteenth-century reminiscences of Kitty Kitchen, published in 1976 by the Herndon Historical Society. Courtesy of J. Berkley Green

The Standard Oil wagon, driven by franchise dealer I. W. Cummings, supplied kerosene in the early 1900s to run steam engines, tractors, and power saws. The company also supplied stores

which had large oil drums from which they sold kerosene by one or five-gallon can quantities to householders to light their lamps and operate space heaters and cookstoves. Courtesy of J. Berkley Green

This funeral procession was on the way to Herndon's Chestnut Grove Cemetery about 1900. It was the first picture of what is now a valuable collection which J. Berkley Green has made over the past thirty-two years. His friend and associate, Herman Kephart, gave him the picture in 1954. Mr. Green hung it on the wall of his funeral parlor, and the public interest was so great that he began to seek out private collections of old Herndon photographs, some of which he copied. He now has over 200 pictures, many of which are on display in the Green Funeral Home. Courtesy of J. Berkley Green

The Harrison mule team and wagon did hauling of all kinds in the Herndon area prior to the time when roads were improved and motorized trucks became generally available. The material transported included firewood, railroad ties, hatchet and axe handles, barrel staves, charcoal, wheat, and hay.

Ausberry Harrison raised mules for sale, breeding jackasses to his mares. About one-third of the work animals in the Herndon area before mechanization were mules. Many farmers considered them more intelligent than horses; they also had more endurance under adverse conditions and required less feed. Courtesy of J. Berkley Green

After rural free delivery was inaugurated in 1896, mail wagons gradually became familiar sights on the roads of Fairfax County. Designed for a two-horse team and built with wide chassis and high wheels, these wagons were intended to assure that neither rain nor snow nor gloom of night prevented the Post Office Department's trusted couriers from the swift completion of their appointed rounds. Shown in this photograph taken about 1915 is the wagon that carried mail between Herndon and Floris. Courtesy of Fairfax County Library Photographic Archive

Robert Schneider operated a hardware store in Herndon for about ten years and E. L. Robey operated his drugstore for about thirty. During Herndon's business district fire in 1917, the hardware store was saved, but Robey's was destroyed. The druggist reestablished his business in an old mill building belonging to Hutcheson and Mitchell.

In the early years of the twentieth century, stores like this sold such a variety of goods that some of them resembled modern shopping centers housed in one building (Schneider, Herndon). Courtesy of J. Berkley Green

172

When federal funds became available through the Public Works Administration during the Depression, Herndon purchased the privately owned Herndon Water Company in 1936 and passed a bond issue to finance a central water and sewer system. A little park adjacent to the station was purchased from the railroad in 1938 and on it the municipal building was erected. It included space for government offices and meeting rooms, as well as the town's post office. In the late 1960s, the post office was moved to its own building about two blocks east on Elden Street (Schug, "Herndon").

There has been a depot in the same place since the Alexandria, Loudoun and Hampshire Railroad was built to Herndon in 1859. This particular structure probably dates from the time the Southern Railway absorbed the line into its system in the 1890s.

Herndon was once the center of a large dairy farming area. In 1907, a statement was published that "no point on either the main line or the Bluemont branch of the Southern Railway ships more milk than Herndon (Fairfax County, Virginia, 1907).

When the Bluemont line was leased from the Southern and renamed the Washington and Old Dominion Railroad, it carried freight, passengers, and especially commuters to and from jobs in Washington for more than forty years (Schug, "Herndon").

In addition to the Herndon Historical Society's museum, the building also houses the Herndon Chamber of Commerce. Richard Netherton photo

Early experiences which appealed to the senses live in the memories of the townspeople. Sounds associated with the first half of this century were the banging of large metal milk cans as men worked on shipments of milk at the depot. The whistles of incoming trains and the noon whistle at the nearby Wiehle lumber mill were familiar sounds on weekdays.

Lottie Dyer Schneider remembered the grove of sixty-foot-tall pine trees at John Barker's residence, The Pines. She wrote: "There was always music in these trees. They sighed softly in gentle breezes, their melodies were more audible when brisk winds blew, and in times of storm they moaned and swayed. They seemed to me like a giant instrument which expressed such varied moods and changing rhythm" (Schneider, Herndon).

Unusual visitors to the town made lasting impressions upon the residents. There was a patent medicine man who sometimes put on a show to sell bottles of his murky liniment. A man who came with a dancing bear on a chain was an

intriguing sight. Another itinerant showman charmed the children with his hand organ and a tiny monkey dressed in a bright suit who scampered through the crowd holding out his hat to beg for pennies. There were also bands of colorful gypsies who came occasionally, camping just outside of the town's corporate limits and telling fortunes for all who would pay.

In this aerial photograph of downtown Herndon taken in the 1950s, one may see buildings which replaced the sixteen businesses and two residences which were burned during Herndon's great fire on March 22, 1917. The Herndon depot and town hall are at the curve in Elden Street as it crosses the old W&OD right-of-way. Courtesy of J. Berkley Green

Donald Levine, a relative newcomer to Herndon, became intrigued with the history of his own residence and wound up spending two-and-one-half years researching and documenting, from basic source records at the courthouse, the history of every square foot of land in Herndon from the proprietary grant in 1649 to at least 1900. It turned out to be a labor of love for the town on whose council he now serves. In the introduction of the 1,500-page study which resulted from this research project, finished in 1982, the author wrote:

Herndon is a special place to me—it is not merely the designation of the area in which my family and I live in our 1868-schoolhouse-converted-into-a-residence home, but much more importantly, a place with character, a place where one single individual can still participate in the town and actually influence the direction of the community, a place where a person can walk at night and feel at ease and at peace with an environment that is unique and not a reproduction of a hundred other communities, a place where one can go into his side yard and feel the quiet, the peace and serenity and the history of many others who have come before and left a legacy which time has not yet eradicated by progress, by uniformity, by conformity, by repetitiveness; Herndon is home.

Courtesy of Fairfax County Library Photographic Archive

The Herndon Fortnightly Club was first organized in 1889 and met every two weeks at the Herndon Seminary. Its principal project was to organize a public library and the initial forty volumes grew to over 1,000. The building in which the collection was stored burned in the great Herndon fire of 1917. After almost ten years of fund raising efforts, the present library building was constructed on Spring Street in 1927. An addition was built in 1953 (Schneider, Herndon).

In 1971, the Herndon Fortnightly Library became a mini-library in Fairfax County's library system and is open most days of the week.

The club still provides funds to purchase gifts for the library's collection. In addition to other community projects, the Fortnightly also awards scholarships to library science graduate students. Richard Netherton photo

When community youth problems loomed large in the mid-1970s, a committee of adults and youthful citizens of Herndon was formed to plan a facility to provide opportunities for constructive and healthful use of leisure time. Priorities were determined and a community center was constructed in 1979 with the help of community block grant funds from Fairfax County. The use of the building has far exceeded expectations, and an addition with racquetball courts, a fitness center, and multipurpose meeting rooms was added in 1985.

The Herndon Parks and Recreation Department administers the community-wide program which includes classes, workshops, dance, drama, arts, crafts, and gymnastics for all ages from preschoolers to senior citizens. Richard Netherton photo

Vienna

Vienna was first called Ayr Hill after Ayreshire, Scotland, birthplace of an early resident, John Hunter. The community grew and in 1857, the U.S. government established the Ayr Hill postal district with Margaret Williams as postmaster.

A new resident of the community who wished to invest in and promote its development suggested changing its name to Vienna after his native town in New York (now Phelps, New York). When the post office name was changed to Vienna in 1862, the developer, William Hendrick, was its first postmaster (Lisbeth, "Post Offices").

The Alexandria, Loudoun and Hampshire Railroad was built through the community to Herndon in the late 1850s. Soon after, when the Civil War began, the first military skirmish involving a railroad occurred with Confederate and Union troops at the Park Street crossing. An engraving depicting the engagement hangs in the town hall.

Vienna was incorporated as a town one-and-a-half miles square in 1890. Through annexation in recent years, Vienna's area has been increased to four and three-tenths square miles. The 1980 U.S. Census counted the population as 15,469, making it the largest incorporated town in the Commonwealth of Virginia.

Map of Vienna from Hopkins' Atlas, 1878

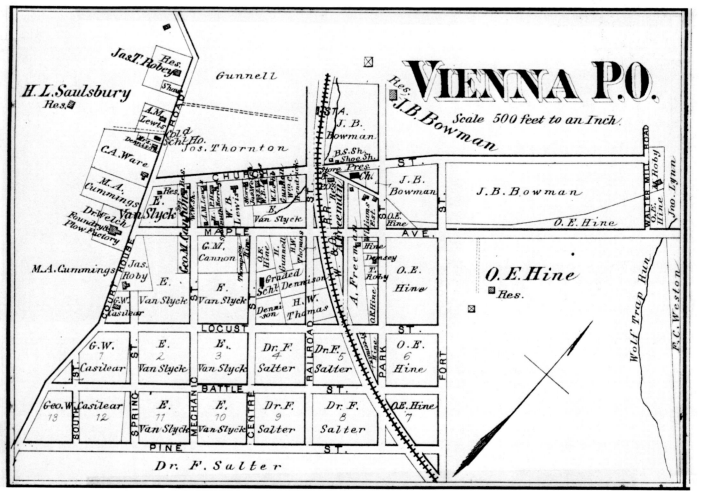

The Freeman House was probably built about 1859 by Abraham Lydecker. His daughter Caroline married Anderson Freeman and the couple later received and lived on the property. The structure has at different times been used as a residence, store, post office, insurance office, and a garage for the town's first fire truck, a 1917 Model T Ford with three sixty-gallon chemical cans.

The town of Vienna purchased the building and grounds in 1969 and has restored it. A country store has been stocked on the main floor; there are living quarters above. On the Virginia Landmarks Register, it is operated as a museum house by Historic Vienna, Inc.

The old Vienna Library, built in 1897 on Library Lane and now the oldest library building in Fairfax County, was moved to the Freeman property in 1969 from the lot now occupied by the Patrick Henry Branch Library. The little Vienna Library has been restored and is now open

the first Sunday of each month so that visitors may see how a focal point of cultural activity for the community appeared in an earlier day. Photo by Marie Kisner; courtesy of the town of Vienna

When Virginia prepared to write a new constitution in 1867, Orrin E. Hine was elected a convention delegate from Fairfax County. He had been a Yankee officer and had returned to the county and Vienna after the Civil War. He was the local agent for the Freedmen's Bureau and provided land for a black church and school on Lawyers Road.

By 1885, Mr. Hine owned 6,440 acres of land including a large farm and a real estate office. One of the community improvements he advocated was the realignment of the main street so that a new Maple Avenue, straighter than Church Street, took its place as the main street through the village.

The town of Vienna was incorporated in 1890 and Mr. Hine was the first mayor. He served in that capacity for ten years. Because of his interest in and efforts on behalf of public education and responsive government, it was said of him by his neighbors "that he has restored to this section more than he destroyed" (Reed, Fairfax County).

This photograph of the Hine home, Pleasant Place, was taken about 1900. It was located behind the present site of the Giant store. Courtesy of the town of Vienna

Johannes Adam Simon Oertel was born in Bavaria and demonstrated talent as a draftsman and artist at a very early age. Although he became an Episcopal clergyman and was throughout his life in charge of several churches, he was also a prolific engraver, painter, and wood carver. Several of his religious paintings are at the National Gallery and the National Cathedral. Toward the end of his productive life, he resided with his son, John Frederick Oertel, in Vienna, where he died in 1909 at the age of eighty-six (Dictionary of American Biography). *Courtesy of Fairfax County Library Photographic Archive*

The Vienna railroad station was remodeled in 1894 after the Southern Railway took over the Washington, Ohio and Western Railroad. It had been the successor to the Alexandria, Loudoun and Hampshire Railroad line which was first completed to Herndon by 1859. The building, as altered, included a freight office, a telegraph office with a ticket window, and a passenger waiting room. The station was heated by three pot-bellied stoves. The water tank, shown to the rear, supplied boilers of the steam trains.

The last train ran in 1968 and subsequently, the tracks were removed. When the Virginia Electric and Power Company purchased the right-of-way from what had become the Washington and Old Dominion Railroad, the power company gave the station to the Town of Vienna. It is currently in use as a club house by the Northern Virginia Model Railroaders, Inc. Courtesy of Ames Williams

Louise Reeves Archer was born in 1893 in Fayetteville, North Carolina. She was graduated from Morgan State Teachers College in Baltimore and taught in North Carolina and at Howard University.

She lived in northwest Washington, D.C., and was married to an architect. For twenty-six years, she commuted to Vienna, first by trolley and train, then by automobile, to serve as principal and fifth-to-seventh grade teacher at the Vienna Colored School. She believed strongly in the value of a formal education and also education in the domestic, industrial, and fine arts, of which she gave her students full measure.

When she organized a 4-H Club at the school in 1936, assigned projects were completed and almost every student in the school had participated. The county agent, H. B. Derr, applauded her efforts: "It is a creditable showing for a colored school that has not received its full share of assistance in club work" (Netherton. Fairfax County).

When Mrs. Archer died suddenly in 1948, parents and students petitioned the school board to change the school's name to honor her. This was accomplished in 1950.

The school was integrated along with all other county public schools in 1959 and since that time has been greatly modernized and enlarged. Courtesy of Fairfax County Library Photographic Archive

In the Vienna station of the Washington and Old Dominion Railroad, Agent-Telegrapher S. D. Ledford presides at his key. When this photograph was taken in June 1933, the railroad was suffering declines in both passenger traffic and shipment of milk and garden produce to the Washington markets. In the fight to keep the railroad operating through the depression years, its employees gave up part of their pay to meet the company's expenses subject to a promise of reimbursement when business improved (Williams, W&OD). From the Glenn Cunningham Collection; courtesy of Ames W. Williams

The old municipal building on the same property was demolished when Vienna built the first unit of the present town hall in 1952. The new building was designed for phase development; additions were made in 1958 and 1964. The town hall houses the council chamber and other meeting rooms, offices, and the police department.

The first councilwoman elected to serve on the town council was Susan J. Swet-nam who was officially sworn in in 1921. Like the men who served with her, because of an unusual provision in Virginia law, she had to sign an oath that she had not, since 1902, fought in a duel, nor would she fight in a duel while she was in office. This particular oath requirement was apparently dropped after 1928 (Patrick Henry Branch Library). Photo by Marie Kisner; courtesy of the town of Vienna

A clear verbal picture of Vienna's schools as they existed seventy-five years ago appeared in a 1907 publication: "Vienna is justly proud of her public schools and can point with pride to the record made by her graduates, who have done her credit in high schools and colleges. Advanced pupils take advantage of the educational opportunities afforded in nearby Washington, and many go there daily." Some of the trolley-riding students went in the other direction when the first high school program was offered in Oakton in 1911 (Fairfax County, Virginia, 1907; Jones, "Oakton School").

From 1872 until construction of the present building in 1921, three schools were located at the site of the Vienna Elementary School on Center Street. The building has had several additions. After World War II, schools were built in rapid succession in the Vienna area to accommodate the children of thousands of young families who moved into the area as the federal government expanded and provided jobs. Freedom Hill opened in 1953; Flint Hill in 1955; Cedar Lane in 1956; Marshall Road in 1961; James Madison High School in 1959; and Thoreau Intermediate in 1960 (Patrick Henry Branch Library files). Drawing by David Paul Skibiak; courtesy of Marie Kisner, town of Vienna

In 1902, Charles Delano Hine, son of Orrin E. Hine, deeded to the town the lot on the southeast corner of Maple Avenue and Center Street to be used for "free schools, free libraries, free baths, free gymnasiums, and other free institutions for the development and enlightenment of a free people." To this site, the Vienna Library was moved from Library Lane in order to be more centrally located in the town.

When the town's population grew rapidly in the 1950s, townspeople applied to the Fairfax County Library Board for a branch in Vienna. After a major fund drive, the Patrick Henry Branch was opened in a store front in the Giant Shopping Center in 1962. The heavy use by the citizens justified a separate building and the old Vienna Library was moved to the Freeman property on Church Street so that the large new library building could be erected on the corner of Maple and Center. The new brick building, designed by architects Beery and Rio, has an architectural lineage that goes back to the early Virginia courthouses. It was opened in 1971 and has maintained a high community usage ever since.

Because the children's librarian loves animals, there was a resident guinea pig in the children's section, and he was much loved by the young patrons. He was so popular that it was necessary to put the following notice on his cage: "Wilbur's mother asks that you not feed him" (Patrick Henry Branch Library). Wilbur lived in the library for more than four years. When he died in 1984 a tiny commemorative brass plaque was mounted in his memory. Richard Netherton photo

179

This group was billed as the Mad Mayor and Wildcat Councilmen when they put on a madcap performance in 1965 as part of the town's anniversary observance in Showcase '75. Vienna was celebrating its incorporation in 1890.

From left to right, in costumes of the turn of the century, are Edward Mitchell, Charles Robinson (now Vienna's mayor), Al Norcross, Martha Pennino (now Centreville District's representative on the Board of Supervisors), Richard Dingman, and Mayor James Martinelli. Courtesy of Patrick Henry Branch Library, Vienna

The Vienna Community Center was opened in April, 1966, the first modern facility of its kind in Fairfax County. Community use was so intensive from the first day that a wing was completed in 1968 to accommodate the program.

The building houses the Office of Parks and Recreation for Vienna, which administers the program of indoor and outdoor recreational activities for the entire town. In addition to a large gymnasium, there are meeting rooms for classes, workshops, civic and social organizations, special events, art, fashion and antique shows, dinners, and receptions.

The grounds were landscaped by the local garden clubs and the parking lot was planned so that many trees were left in place to provide welcome shade and an attractive parklike area around the building. Richard Netherton photo

Clifton

Clifton, situated in the deep green valley of Popes Head Creek, was first platted as a town by the County Surveyor in 1869. The land was bisected by the Orange and Alexandria Railroad, now known as the main line south of the Norfolk Southern Railway. A station named Devereux had been established previously at the same location during the Civil War when the Union Army took charge of the trackage and rolling stock of the O & A as part of their U.S. Military Railroad system. The depot was a loading point for firewood which was cut in the vicinity to be used as fuel for the boilers since coal was almost impossible to obtain.

Following the Civil War, the earlier Dye's Mill post office which had operated at Union Mills on Bull Run was closed and a new post office was opened at the Devereux Station location. It was named Clifton after Clifton Springs, New York, with Harrison G. Otis, a native of New York State, appointed postmaster in 1869.

Official town status was acquired in 1902 as a square with a total area of one-quarter square mile, making it one of the smallest municipalities in the state. Each October thousands of visitors come to Clifton Day to walk around the little, old-fashioned town, eat a barbecued meal out-of-doors, and shop for bargains at the many booths set up for the occasion.

The population was recorded as 170 in the 1980 U.S. Census.

Excerpt from Clifton area map from Hopkins' Atlas, *1878*

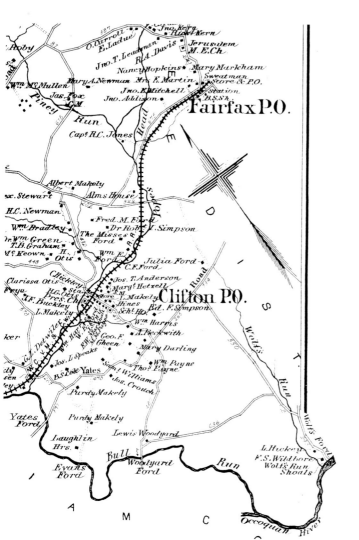

Annie Elgin, seated on the right, and her sister Helen, seated on the left, about 1906. Both taught for many years at the Clifton School, were active members of the Clifton Baptist Church, and were Worthy Matrons of Clifton's branch of the Order of the Eastern Star.

Annie married Henry Farnham Adair and Helen married Charles Robert Buckley. Copy by William Edmund Barrett

Clifton appeared in guidebooks at the turn of the century as a resort. The Paradise Springs northeast of town were not deemed significant enough to list among the famous spas and springs of Virginia. More than one enterprising individual planned to bottle and market the healthful spring water commercially. Mrs. Mary Merwin ordered two railroad boxcar loads of these bottles in 1910 and built a bottling plant. The effort eventually ended in bankruptcy. Virginia Ruck photo

The first Clifton High School, built on Main Street, was also the first high school in Fairfax County. It served the town until 1912, when a new combined high school and elementary school bulding was erected on the hill overlooking Clifton. This second wooden structure was taken down and replaced by a brick building in 1953. The first structure, shown here, after being used as an Odd Fellows Hall for a number of years, was demolished in 1978. Painting by Gerald Hennesy; used with permission of the artist

Many young people in Clifton had summer jobs at the farm and canning factory of Mr. and Mrs. J. Lovell Fristoe. The buildings are still in use at the end of Chapel Street on the edge of town. Fristoe operated the grocery store across from Buckley Brothers, now the Clifton Superette, about 1906. Courtesy of Helen Buckley and the Clifton Betterment Association

Most of the buildings shown in this aerial photo of Clifton taken about 1936 are still standing. One exception is the railroad station between Buckley Brothers' Store—"everything from a pin to a plow"—and the Southern Railway tracks, center left of the picture. It was closed in 1956. The tar-papered gold ore reduction plant, which figured strongly in a gold mine hoax perpetrated by several enterprising individuals during the Depression, still stands across the tracks a little above where the old depot stood. A few buildings have been added in recent years with such restraint that they have not disturbed the homey atmosphere of the tiny railroad town. Courtesy of Helen E. Buckley

Clifton's Volunteer Fire Department was formed in 1942 due, at least in part, to discovery that the town's blacksmith made a practice of throwing hot ashes on the wooden floor of the blacksmith shed attached to his residence. Prior to this time, Clifton relied on neighborhood bucket brigades and, in the event of a major fire, equipment from Fairfax or Vienna. Here, trucks are pumping water from Popes Head Creek during a call to assist Clifton in the 1930s. The truck in the center of the road was acquired by Fairfax from Falls Church and was the first fire truck to serve the Clifton area. Courtesy of Alfred A. Savia, Deputy Chief, Fairfax County Fire and Rescue Services

The Clifton Volunteer Fire Department was established as an auxiliary unit to the Fairfax County department in 1942. It was chartered as an independent company in 1951. As more and more residents took daytime jobs in Fairfax County and in Washington, however, fewer people were available to answer emergency fire calls. In 1969, by agreement with the county's Fire and Rescue Service, Clifton relinquished control and the unit became Company 16. The boat shown is used for water rescue at Burke Lake, the Potomac, or Occoquan when needed.

The building, in addition to housing firefighting and rescue equipment and personnel, also provides space for many community activities including town meetings, dinners, dances, plays, and luncheons for the annual Clifton House and Garden Tour in the spring. Courtesy of Fairfax County Library Photographic Archive

This small town streetscape on Chapel Road was photographed in 1968 prior to major restoration efforts in Clifton. Fences have been replaced and building additions have been made since.

The residences have often been called by the names of their owners in the nineteenth and first half of the twentieth centuries. Former mayor Julian Burke's house is at the far left, next to the Payne house. At the end of the road in the middle of the picture, on Main Street, is the Quigg house. To the right of it on Chapel is the Detwiler house; at the far right is the Woodyard house. Since 1979 the distinctive character of Clifton's buildings has been preserved by their designation as a historic district. William Edmund Barrett photo

Brigadier General Willard Webb received his promotion to the rank just as his book, Crucial Moments of the Civil War, *was published in 1961. His wife, Margaret Detwiler, was a Clifton native and for most of their adult lives they made the little town their home. He served in the Pacific Theater in World War II. After the war, as a civilian, he was for many years head of the Library of Congress Stacks Division. Many of his religious wood carvings adorn the interior walls of the Clifton Presbyterian Church. Courtesy of Margaret Webb and the Clifton Betterment Association*

Major General Cunningham Bryant was born in Clifton in 1921 and grew up on Ford Lane in what had been the Mayhugh House. His mother was a schoolteacher from South Boston and taught in the Clifton "colored elementary school." His father was a section hand on the Southern Railway and obtained a pass so that his son could attend Shaw Junior High School and Cardozo High School in Washington, D.C.

General Bryant was an infantry officer in the European Theater during World War II. Afterwards, he attended the Army's War College and Command and General Staff School. A member of the D. C. National Guard, he was made its commanding general by presidential appointment in 1971 and thus became the first federally recognized black general officer in the National Guard. He was promoted to the rank of major general in 1975. Courtesy of D. C. National Guard and Clifton Betterment Association

The hitching post next to the old Buckley Brothers' Store is still in use. Many horses and ponies are raised or boarded in the area around Clifton. This has been a local tradition since former President Ulysees S. Grant boarded his two fine Arabian stallions, Leopard and Linden Tree, at the Springdale Farm about 1887. The two had been presented to Grant in 1880 as a mark of esteem by the Sultan of Turkey.

Numerous Arabians and thoroughbreds are raised for showing, racing, and stud service within a mile of the Clifton town limits. The champion racers have had names like Jon-San Nova, Commanding Kathy, I'm Clifton, and Mayor Swem. Virginia Ruck photo

These Cub Scouts successfully completed a photographic essay project on a day in the life of kids in Clifton. Here they indulge in typical boyish antics in front of Earl Lee's Superette grocery store. The double track of the Southern Railway's main line south and the old dilapidated Clifton Hotel can be seen in the background. Virginia Ruck photo

Six leaders of the Town of Clifton about 1910, and their occupations. Seated, left to right, are G. B. Wright, lumberman; G. H. Wine, Sr., builder; and "Grand-pap Gustie" Mayhugh, operator of an oasis by the railroad described as "a genteel and orderly bar." Standing, left to right, are Winter Marshall, lumberman; R. M. Kivett, butcher, grocer, journalist, real estate developer, and former mayor of Clifton; and young Vernon Wright. Several were members of the Masonic Lodge. Copy by Ronald Petersen; courtesy of Mrs. Helen E. Buckley

Five Clifton gentlemen in 1982, members of the Clifton Gentlemen's Club, relax outside the Hungry Mouth Cafe behind a pot of steaming hot chili. Left to right, Lee Ruck, Joe Bertoni, Rick Dygve, "Mac" Arnold, and Earl Lee. Tracy Woodward photo; courtesy of the Fairfax Journal

Reston

Reston, a "new town" in the Old Dominion, was first designed in 1962. The concept and the initial funding for the 7,000 acres of land were provided by Robert E. Simon, Jr., whose initials plus the English suffix for town form its name. In 1967 Gulf Oil, one of the investors in the development, took it over from Simon, for the most part adhering to his concepts for an environmentally conscious live/work/play community. Mobil Corporation purchased the remaining 3,400 acres of undeveloped land from Gulf in 1978. It is the plan of their subsidiary company, Reston Land Corporation, to complete the building of the community by the 1990s, at which time the resident population is expected to be between 70,000 and 80,000.

The land on which this innovative concept is being developed was once part of Thomas, Sixth Lord Fairfax's Great Falls Manor. After the land left Fairfax family ownership, Dr. C. A. Max Wiehle of Philadelphia bought part of it and had a town designed on the drawing board with streets, parks, and an industrial area which would provide jobs for the residents. Wiehle received its charter from the Virginia Assembly in 1898. Dr. Wiehle planned to make it a health resort and a summer retreat for Washingtonians who would come out on the Alexandria, Loudoun and Hampshire Railroad, from 1894 the Southern Railway.

The Restonians, as they call themselves, have a strong sense of community and have worked over the years through committees and boards in their organizations and with the county officials to plan and build a community center, improve roads and bridges, and to resolve many issues of local importance. The community does not have a town or city government charter but is considered a part of Fairfax County.

Although Reston is an unincorporated community, it has specific boundaries encompassing an area of approximately eleven and one-half square miles. The population in the 1980 U.S. Census was over 35,000.

*A*n aerial view of Reston's first Village Center, Lake Anne, designed by the New York architectural firm of Conklin and Rossant. The townhouses of Waterview Cluster are in the foreground; the highrise building is Heron House; Washington Plaza has apartments over first floor shops; Lake Anne Office Building is behind them; and Fellowship House I for senior citizens is the white highrise to the left above center of the photograph. Lake Anne is a manmade lake on Colvin Run. The Lake Anne Historic District was established in 1984. Courtesy of Reston Land Corporation

*R*obert E. Simon purchased land formerly known as Wiehle and Sunset Hills in 1961 with the proceeds from his sale of Carnegie Hall in New York City. He worked with Fairfax County officials to design a new ordinance which would make possible his plan for clustering dwelling units in order to leave large areas of open space for trees, meadows, and park lands. He planned a commercial/professional/industrial area which was to be developed so that people who lived in Reston could also work there and not have to commute to jobs in Washington. The number of jobs being provided by Reston is now approximately one per household in a rapidly expanding high technology development of the industrial property (Netherton, "Reston"). Portrait courtesy of Hunters Woods Regional Library

The area around Isaac Newton Square, shown in the top right corner, illustrates the skillful planning of open space to enhance both the convenience and amenity of development in Reston. The square houses offices, laboratories, light industry, a racquet club, and fast food shops. At the lower left are the residential units of Golf Course Island Cluster, designed to maximize the effect of the landscaped spaces separating these units. Between this cluster and the square, a golf course serves both as a recreation facility and as a major open space feature of the community. Courtesy of Reston Land Corporation

The national headquarters of the U.S. Geological Survey (USGS) is located in this $50 million complex in the Reston Center for Business, Government and Industry, a 103-acre site along the Dulles Airport Access Road in western Fairfax County. The Geological Survey moved to the site eighteen miles from Washington in 1973 as part of the federal government's effort to decentralize many of its agencies. In its present location in Reston, the USGS building provides a million square feet of floor space for the world's largest earth science library, modern geological and hydrological laboratories, and a topographic mapping plant. The buildings shown here are designed in the distinctive shape of the compass rose that traditionally has been the mapmaker's hallmark. Courtesy of Reston Land Corporation

The Reston International Center, built in 1973, exemplifies the modern trend for conference centers located out of the central city on sites designed specifically to serve their needs and close to air and highway travel facilities. This self-contained center attracts a worldwide variety of meetings and special events throughout the year. Courtesy of Reston Land Corporation

*L*ocated immediately east of the Reston International Center, along the Dulles Airport Access Road, a twenty-seven-acre condominium houses the national headquarters of some of the nation's most important ''think tanks'' in the field of education. Shown here, reading clockwise, are the buildings of the Council for Exceptional Children, the Art Education Association (under construction), the Distributive Education Clubs of America, the National Council of Teachers of Mathematics, National Association of Secondary School Principals, and the Music Educators National Conference. Courtesy of Reston Land Corporation

*W*arner Amex Cable Television, in operation by the early 1970s, serves Reston and was the first cable system in Fairfax County. Community and local origination programs are part of its overall presentation to subscribers. This crew is taping the Annual Reston Festival at Lake Anne Village Center. Marvin Simms photo; courtesy of Warner Amex Cable

*R*obert E. Simon spoke at the dedication of the Reston Community Center in May 1979. The building, which cost $2.6 million, is located in Hunters Woods Village Center, next to Fellowship House II. In addition to a staff to operate the complex and well-attended program, the center houses a 275-seat theater, an Olympic-size pool, arts and crafts areas, meeting rooms, a large community hall with kitchen, rehearsal rooms, a dark room, and a woodworking shop. Warren Mattox photo; courtesy of Reston Land Corporation

The Terraset—set into the ground—Elementary School opened in Reston in 1977. The architects of this innovative underground educational building received a national design award for their concept integrating educational, conservation, and ecological goals. The solar energy collectors were funded by Saudi Arabia. A similar school, Terra-Centre, was built in Burke Centre in 1980. Exterior photo by Richard Netherton, interior photo by Abbie Edwards

Reston shares America's traditional fondness for parades. Part of South Lakes High School's award-winning marching band forms up to step off in the community's annual Halloween Parade. Other marchers in their costumes wait on the side ready to fall in and march. An impromptu parade winds its way along the road to welcome home one of Reston's residents, John Graves, following his release as an Iranian hostage in 1980. Abbie Edwards photo

This aerial photo gives a good overview of the open space and planning which has gone into the Reston "new town" development. The proximity of Dulles International Airport, at the top of the picture, demonstrates a promise for future growth, due to the transportation potential. The Dulles Airport Access Road winds its way through the development and became a wider ribbon when it was widened to eight lanes with a newly state-authorized toll road, giving quicker access to and from Tysons Corner and Washington, D.C.

Reston has been able to attract high technology firms like GTE, Sperry, Tandem, and Advanced Technology to its industrial park and life style. It has played a significant part in Fairfax County's leadership in high technology on the East Coast since 1980.

Of the associations which have selected Fairfax County for the location of their national headquarters, 27 percent have chosen Reston. Blue Ridge Aerial Surveys photo

Gentlemen anglers, fishing from their raft in Reston's Lake Thoreau, enjoy the warmth of early spring sunshine. Reston's master plan called for developing a series of manmade lakes to serve the needs for recreation, conservation, environmental quality, and natural life style. Abbie Edwards photo

*Fairfax County flag waving in front of
the Massey Building*

CHAPTER

11

An Anniversary View

In 1976, the year America celebrated the bicentennial of its independence, the Fairfax County Office of Comprehensive Planning in cooperation with the Fairfax County History Commission undertook to document the county's history through a photographic view of its people and their activities. One of the commission's members uniquely qualified to do this was Bernard N. Boston, then Chief Photographer of the *Washington Star*, one-time president of the White House Press Photographer's Association, and recipient of numerous honors and awards for excellence in photography. Drawing from many parts of the county and watching its residents at work and play, Boston compiled a collection of 121 photographs which was titled "Fairfax County at 1976." From this pictorial essay, which is now part of the Photographic Archive of Fairfax County, housed in the Virginia Room of the Fairfax County Public Library, twenty-three have been selected. These scenes offer an anniversary view of Fairfax County, presented in terms of the most important and interesting of the county's resources—its people.

Several of the pictures in Bernie Boston's photographic essay were placed in a bicentennial time capsule which was deposited in the county courthouse complex to be opened in the year 2076.

Bernard N. Boston, self portrait

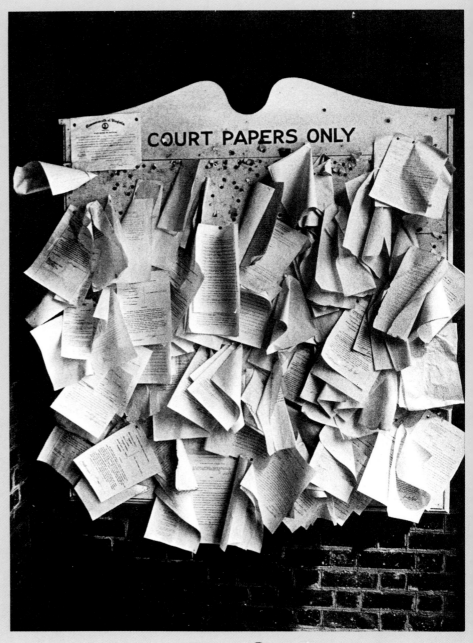

Court notices posted at the door of the old courthouse

Voting in a Dranesville District precinct

Fairfax County police officers working a traffic detail

Fairfax County fireman battles a blaze in Annandale

English class for foreign students at Langley High School, McLean; Sharon Klompus (kneeling) is the teacher

Trash collection at James Fenimore Cooper Intermediate School parking lot, a free county service every Saturday

Pat and Bill Vorndick's country wedding on a farm near Chantilly

Waiting at Tysons Corner Shopping Mall

Tysons Corner Shopping Mall

*Pizza, the staff of life for all kinds of
county folks in 1976*

Roadside produce vendor, Leesburg Pike near Herndon

Flea market on Chain Bridge Road, McLean

Waiting at Lorton

Reading at Fairfax City Regional Library

Watching at Lake Fairfax

Sunning at Great Falls

Ice skating at dusk, McLean

Soccer

*R*ush hour traffic on the Beltway (I-495) near Tysons Corner

*B*ritish Airways and Air France Concordes in front of the terminal at Dulles International Airport

Winter scene in horse country

Bibliography

Substantial collections of publications, pictures, maps, manuscripts, and selected public records relating to the history of Fairfax County and the communities within it may be found in the local history rooms of the Fairfax County Public Library and the public libraries of the cities of Alexandria and Falls Church. Specialized research collections exist at Mount Vernon and Gunston Hall, and continuing programs of local history research are carried on by the Fairfax County Office of Comprehensive Planning, Fairfax County History Commission, Historical Society of Fairfax County, Falls Church Historical Commission, and George Mason University. All of these sources contributed information used in this book, and they are recommended to readers who wish to go further in their research. The specific references that are noted in the captions of this book are as follows:

Books

Abbot, W. W., and Twohig, D., eds. *The Papers of George Washington.* Charlottesville: University Press of Virginia, 1981—

Acts of the General Assembly. Richmond: Commonwealth of Virginia.

Alves, Joseph H., and Spelman, H. *Near the Falls: Two Hundred Years of The Falls Church.* Falls Church, Va.: The Falls Church, 1969.

Anderson, Ellen. *Salona, Fairfax County, Virginia.* Fairfax: Fairfax County Office of Comprehensive Planning, 1979.

Beirne, Rosamond. *William Buckland.* Baltimore: Maryland Historical Society, 1958.

Biographical Directory of the American Congress, 1774-1971. Senate Document No. 92-8. Washington: United States Government Printing Office, 1971.

Cooling, B. Franklin. *Historical Highlights of the Bull Run Regional Park.* Fairfax: Fairfax County Office of Comprehensive Planning, 1971.

Cooling, B. Franklin. *Symbol, Sword and Shield: Defending Washington During the Civil War.* Hamden, Conn.: Archon Books, 1975.

Curran, Louise. *McLean Remembers Again.* McLean, Va.: The Sound Publications, 1976.

Dabney, Virginius. *Virginia: The New Dominion.* Garden City, N.Y.: Doubleday and Company, 1971.

DaCosta, B., ed. *Historic Homes of America: An American Heritage Guide.* New York: American Heritage Publishing Company, 1971.

DiBacco, Thomas. *Moorefield: Home of Early Baptist Preacher Jeremiah Moore.* Fairfax: Fairfax County Office of Comprehensive Planning, 1971.

Douglas, Henry. *Falls Church: Places and People.* Falls Church, Va.: Falls Church Historical Commission, 1981.

Eskew, Garnett L. *Willard's of Washington.* New York: Coward-McCann, Inc., 1954.

Evans, D'Anne. *Wakefield Chapel.* Fairfax: Fairfax County Office of Comprehensive Planning, 1977.

Fairfax County Board of Supervisors. *Industrial and Historical Sketch of Fairfax County, Virginia.* Falls Church, Va.: Newell, 1907.

Fairfax County Citizens Handbook. Fairfax: Fairfax County Office of Public Affairs, 1980.

Fairfax County Directory: A Civic-Government Handbook. Vienna, Va.: Fairfax County Federation of Citizens Associations, 1957.

Fairfax County in Virginia, Being a Random Selection From Some Rare Sources, 1742-1973. Fairfax: Fairfax County Office of Comprehensive Planning, 1974.

Fairfax County Historic Landmarks Survey. Historic American Buildings Survey. Fairfax: Fairfax County Office of Comprehensive Planning, 1969—. (OCP-HABSI).

Fitzpatrick, John C., ed. *The Diaries of George Washington, 1748-1799.* 4 vols. Boston: Houghton-Mifflin Co., 1925.

Fitzpatrick, John C., ed. *The Writings of George Washington From Original Manuscript Sources, 1745-1799.* 39 vols. Washington: Government Printing Office, 1931-1944.

Freeman, Douglas S. *George Washington: A Biography.* 6 vols. New York: Charles Scribner's Sons, 1948-1954.

Gamble, Robert. *Sully, The Biography of a House.* Chantilly, Va.: Sully Foundation, Ltd., 1973.

Gutheim, Frederick. *The Potomac.* New York: Rinehart and Company, 1940.

Harriot, Thomas. *A Brief and True Report of the New Found Land of Virginia.* 1590. Reprint. New York: Dover Publications, 1972.

Harrison, Fairfax. *Landmarks of Old Prince William.* 1924. Reprint. Berryville, Va.: Chesapeake Book Company, 1944.

Harwood, H. H., Jr. *Rails to the Blue Ridge.* Privately printed, undated.

Hopkins, G. M. *Atlas of Fifteen Miles Around Washington Including the Counties of Fairfax and Alexandria, Virginia.* Philadelphia: G. M. Hopkins, 1879.

Jones, Virgil C. *First Manassas: The Story of the Bull Run Campaign.* Gettysburg, Pa.: Civil War Times Illustrated, 1973.

Kilmer, Kenton, and Sweig, Donald. *The Fairfax Family in Fairfax County.* Fairfax: Fairfax County Office of Comprehensive Planning, 1975.

Kinnaird, Clark. *George Washington: A Pictorial Biography.* New York: Hastings House, 1967.

Lankford, John, ed. *Captain John Smith's America.* Harper Torchbooks, New York: Harper and Row, 1967.

McLean Community Center Handbook. McLean, Va.: McLean Community Center Foundation, 1975.

Mitchell, Beth. *Beginning at a White Oak: Patents and Northern Neck Grants in Fairfax County, Virginia.* Fairfax: Fairfax County Office of Comprehensive Planning, 1977.

Mount Vernon Ladies' Association of the Union. *Annual Report,* 1965.

Netherton, Nan. *Clifton: Brigadoon in Virginia.* Clifton, Va.: Clifton Betterment Assn., 1980.

Netherton, Nan. *Montebello at Mount Eagle.* Alexandria, Va.: Montebello Associates, 1982.

Netherton, Nan, and Grundset, Eric. *Catalog of the Photographic Archive of Fairfax County.* Fairfax: Fairfax County History Commission, 1981.

Netherton, Nan; Sweig, Donald; Artemel, Janice; Hickin, Patricia; and Reed, Patrick. *Fairfax County, Virginia: A History.* Fairfax: Fairfax County Board of Supervisors, 1978.

Netherton, Ross. *The Colvin Run Mill.* Fairfax: Fairfax County Office of Comprehensive Planning, 1976.

Netherton, Ross and Nan. *Green Spring Farm, Fairfax County.* Fairfax: Fairfax County Office of Comprehensive Planning, 1970.

Netherton, Ross, and Waldeck, Ruby. *The Fairfax County Courthouse.* Fairfax: Fairfax County Office of Comprehensive Planning, 1977.

O'Neal, William B. *Architecture in Virginia.* New York: Walker and Co., 1968.

Opstad, Donald. *The History of the Fairfax Hunt, 1929-1972.* Fairfax: The Fairfax Hunt, 1972.

Petersilia, Martin, and Wright, Russell. *Hope Park and Hope Park Mill.* Fairfax: Fairfax County Office of Comprehensive Planning, 1978.

Poland, Charles P., Jr. *Dunbarton, Dranesville, Virginia.* Fairfax: Fairfax County Office of Comprehensive Planning, 1974.

Pryor, Elizabeth. *Frying Pan Farm.* Fairfax: Fairfax County Office of Comprehensive Planning, 1979.

Quarles, Garland. *George Washington and Winchester, Virginia, 1748-1758.* Winchester, Va.: Winchester-Frederick County Historical Society, 1974.

Rafuse, Diane. *Maplewood.* Fairfax: Fairfax County Office of Comprehensive Planning, 1970.

Rust, Jeanne J. *A History of the Town of Fairfax.* Washington: Moore and Moore, Inc., 1960.

Rodrigues, Jeanne, and Hammond, William. *St. Mary's, Fairfax Station, Virginia.* Fairfax Station, Va.: Privately printed, 1975.

Rutland, Robert A., ed. *The Papers of George Mason, 1725-1792.* Chapel Hill: The University of North Carolina Press, 1970.

Schneider, Lottie Dyer. *Memories of Herndon, Virginia.* Radford, Va.: Commonwealth Press, 1962.

Smith, Eugenia. *Centreville, Virginia: Its History and Architecture.* Fairfax: Fairfax County Office of Comprehensive Planning 1973.

Smith, Captain John. *The Generall Historie of Virginia, New-England and the Summer Isles.* 1624. Reprint. Cleveland: The World Publishing Company, 1966.

Snowden, William. *Some Old Historic Landmarks of Virginia and Maryland.* Alexandria, Va.: G. H. Ramsay & Son, 1901.

Sprouse, Edith M. *Colchester: Colonial Port on the Potomac.* Fairfax: Fairfax County Office of Comprehensive Planning, 1975.

Sprouse, Edith M. *Mount Air, Fairfax County, Virginia.* Fairfax: Fairfax County Office of Comprehensive Planning, 1970.

State Historical Markers of Virginia. Richmond: Virginia Department of Conservation and Development, 1948.

Steadman, Melvin L., Jr. *Falls Church By Fence and Fireside.* Falls Church, Va.: Falls Church Public Library, 1964.

Stephenson, Richard. *The Cartography of Northern Virginia.* Fairfax: Fairfax County Office of Comprehensive Planning, 1981.

Stern, Philip, ed. *Soldier Life in the Union and Confederate Armies.* Civil War Centennial Series. Bloomington: Indiana University Press, 1961.

Sweig, Donald, and David, Elizabeth. *A Fairfax Friendship.* Fairfax: Fairfax County Office of Comprehensive Planning, 1982.

Sydnor, Charles. *American Revolutionaries in the Making. Political Activities in Washington's Virginia.* New York: Collier Books, 1952.

Tatham, William. *An Historical and Practical Essay on the Culture and Commerce of Tobacco.* 1800.

Templeman, Eleanor Lee, and Netherton, Nan. *Northern Virginia Heritage.* Arlington, Va.: Privately printed, 1966.

Thane, Elswyth. *Mount Vernon is Ours.* New York: Duell, Sloan and Pearce, 1966.

Tilp, Frederick. *This Was Potomac River.* Arlington: Privately printed, 1978.

Virginia: A Guide to the Old Dominion. American Guides Series, Virginia Writers Program. New York: Oxford, 1941.

Wayland, John. *The Bowmans: A Pioneering Family.* Staunton, Va.: The McClure Co., 1943.

Williams, Ames. *Washington and Old Dominion Railroad, 1847-1968.* Springfield, Va.: Capital Traction Quarterly, 1970.

Wrenn, Tony P. *Cherry Hill.* Falls Church: Falls Church Historical Commission, 1971.

Wrenn, Tony P. *Huntley: A Mason Family Country House.* Fairfax: Fairfax County Office of Comprehensive Planning, 1971.

Wrenn, Tony P. *Falls Church: History of a Virginia Village.* Falls Church, Va.: Falls Church Historical Commission, 1972.

Wrenn, Tony P.; Peters, Virginia; and Sprouse, Edith M. *Legato School, A Centennial Souvenir.* Fairfax: Fairfax County History Commission, 1976.

Newspapers and Periodicals

Andrews, Marshall. "History of Railroads in Fairfax County." Historical Society of Fairfax County *Yearbook*, 3(1954).

Bowman, A. Smith, Jr. "A History of Sunset Hills Farm." Historical Society of Fairfax County *Yearbook*, 6(1958-1959).

Eldridge, Richard. "The Joys of Life at Camp Alger." *Fairfax Chronicles*, 5(Nov. 1981-Jan. 1982).

Heite, Edward. "Scientist on the Bridge." *Virginia Cavalcade*, 15 (Spring 1966) 4.

Johnson, William. "Clean, Clear Water Again Comes to Falls Church." *The Ironworker*, 14(1950).

Jones, Helen Rector. "A History of the Oakton School." Historical Society of Fairfax County *Yearbook*, 7 (1960-1961).

Lisbeth, Robert. "Fairfax County Post Offices and Postmasters, 1774-1890." Historical Society of Fairfax County *Yearbook*, 14 (1976-1977).

Netherton, Nan. "Three Northern Virginians." *Northern Virginia Country,* First Edition, 1976.

Netherton, Nan. "To Know His Brother Better." *Fairfax Chronicles*, 1 (Summer 1977) 3.

"Police Story Told." *The Times* (Springfield, Va.) 10 (30) 4.

Pugh, Evelyn L. "Suffrage Prisoners at the Occoquan Workhouse." *Northern Virginia Heritage*, 1 (1979).

Risley, Paul, and Dahlin, Constance. "A History of New Alexandria, Virginia, Before the Automobile." Historical Society of Fairfax County *Yearbook*, 15 (1978-1979).

"Route 193 Designated State's First 'Byway'." *Virginia Outdoors*, August 1974.

Sprouse, Edith M. "The Last of Washington's Companions." *Fairfax County Bicentennial Newsletter*, December 1976.

Unpublished Papers

Dickey, John. Study of the Objectives and Adaptive Use Restoration of Cherry Hill for the City of Falls Church, Virginia. June 11, 1973. Multilithed.

Fairfax County Office of Comprehensive Planning, Historic American Buildings Survey Inventory forms, 1969—.

McNair, Wilson. What I Remember. Unpublished manuscript in possession of Mrs. Louise McNair Ryder. Multilithed.

Netherton, Nan. Reston: "New Town" in the Old Dominion. Manuscript. Reston Land Corporation, 1984.

Schug, Rita. The Town of Herndon. Paper prepared at George Mason University, May 1973. Photocopy.

Index

Nan and Ross Netherton moved to Northern Virginia in 1951, and promptly began collecting, writing and recording the area's history. They have collaborated in writing about Fairfax County landmarks, and in 1978, Nan directed and contributed to the writing of an 800-page history of Fairfax County. During a decade as historian for the county's Office of Comprehensive Planning, she also headed the inventorying of historic buildings and the creation of a photo archive.

Currently, Nan serves as Executive Director of the Northern Virginia Association of Historians, and is an advisor to the Fairfax County History Commission. Ross is retired from a career as law professor, legislative counsel, and research director. He is active as a member of the Historical Commission of the city of Falls Church, and of professional committees on historic preservation law.

Marcus Cunliffe, who wrote the book's foreword, is a distinguished British historian with a special interest in the United States. Currently a professor of American Studies at The George Washington University, he is the author of *George Washington: Man and Monument*, among other books on American leaders and literature.

Bernard Boston's photographic essay on Fairfax County was done at the time of the Bicentennial of American Independence. He was then chief photographer for the *Washington Star*, and twice president of the White House Photographers' Association. Winner of numerous national awards for his photographs, he currently is on the Washington staff of the *Los Angeles Times*.

Colvin Run Mill

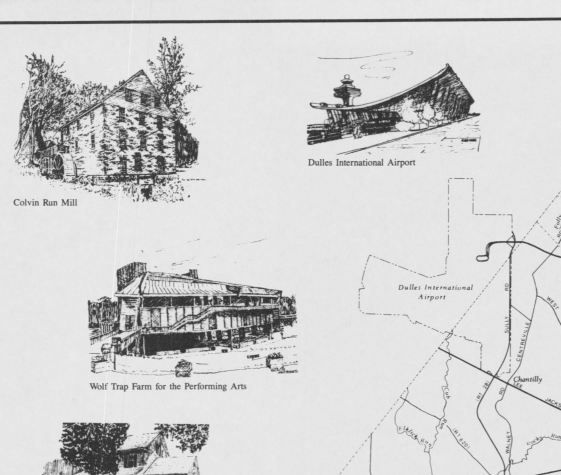

Dulles International Airport

Wolf Trap Farm for the Performing Arts

Sully Plantation

Saint Mary's Church

Bull Run Stone Bridge

Gunston Hall

Reston